Nellwyn Lampert

EVERY BOY I EVER KISSED

a memoir

DUNDURN
TORONTO

Cover illustration: Sophie Paas-Lang
Printer: Webcom, a division of Marquis Printing Inc.

Library and Archives Canada Cataloguing in Publication

Title: Every boy I ever kissed : a memoir / Nellwyn Lampert.
Names: Lampert, Nellwyn, 1990- author.
Description: Includes bibliographical references.
Identifiers: Canadiana (print) 20190119586 | Canadiana (ebook) 20190119616 | ISBN
    9781459745636 (softcover) | ISBN 9781459745643 (PDF) | ISBN 9781459745650 (EPUB)
Subjects: LCSH: Lampert, Nellwyn, 1990- | LCSH: Women—Sexual behavior. | LCSH:
    Women—Sexual behavior—Social aspects. | LCSH: Sex—Social aspects.
Classification: LCC HQ29 .L36 2019 | DDC 306.7082—dc23

1   2   3   4   5   23   22   21   20   19

We acknowledge the support of the **Canada Council for the Arts**, which last year invested $153 million to bring the arts to Canadians throughout the country, and the **Ontario Arts Council** for our publishing program. We also acknowledge the financial support of the **Government of Ontario**, through the **Ontario Book Publishing Tax Credit** and **Ontario Creates**, and the **Government of Canada**.

Nous remercions le **Conseil des arts du Canada** de son soutien. L'an dernier, le Conseil a investi 153 millions de dollars pour mettre de l'art dans la vie des Canadiennes et des Canadiens de tout le pays.

Care has been taken to trace the ownership of copyright material used in this book. The author and the publisher welcome any information enabling them to rectify any references or credits in subsequent editions.

The publisher is not responsible for websites or their content unless they are owned by the publisher.

Printed and bound in Canada.

VISIT US AT

 dundurn.com | 🐦 @dundurnpress | f dundurnpress | 📷 dundurnpress

Dundurn
3 Church Street, Suite 500
Toronto, Ontario, Canada
M5E 1M2

To the Boys

AUTHOR NOTE

This is a true story. The events in this book are all told as they are remembered by the author, without invention or embellishment. In some cases, names, personal details, and slight chronological elements have been altered to protect the privacy of those concerned.

A NOTE ON VIRGINITY

Growing up as a heterosexual woman, I felt that "virginity loss" *for me* would mean having penetrative intercourse. This understanding might not feel right or inclusive to everyone. I encourage you to define virginity however it feels best to you — or to reject the concept altogether!

INTRODUCTION

I COULD ALREADY SEE the morning headlines: *Twenty-Year-Old Virgin Found Dead in Mysterious Field Five Minutes from Home.*

It was dark, but not particularly late, on a spring evening as I followed my roommate Jess away from campus and toward unexplored avenues of urban development. If I'd been back in my hometown, this would have felt completely benign, but this was the big city and our neighbourhood had a very bad reputation.

"Just trust me," Jess said we walked deeper into an unlit field.

"What's in the bag?" I asked, but got no reply.

At the time, the chance of us being murdered that night seemed about as likely as the chance that I would wind up an eighty-year-old virgin cat lady. Which is to say: Very Likely.

I followed Jess to where the field ended on the edge of a construction site. We stopped on a precipice and looked out over a deep cavernous gorge where back-hoes and dump trucks slumbered. My friend reached into her bag and pulled out a stack of white dinner plates.

"I think you need this," she said, handing me an orange Sharpie. "You're going to write everything that's bothering you on these plates and then we're going to smash them!"

I almost cried.

I took the Sharpie and cramped my handwriting in tiny letters across the porcelain plates, worried I would run out of room. I wrote about every boy I'd ever kissed and every ridiculous, unexpected, and shocking moment that had brought me to the edge of that cliff.

. . . . .

Ethan lies crying in the gutter at three in the morning, the back of his coat wet with rainwater that hasn't yet made its way to the sewer. His phone keeps ringing in my purse, but I know what his brother's voice would say on the other end. "It's okay," I keep saying. "Just get up and we'll go home. We'll break up and you'll meet a nice guy; you just have to get out of the street first." I want to scream, I want to cry, I want to drag him up by his collar and force his feet to walk, but I can't. I must be patient, patient, and more patient.

. . . . .

Something isn't right. Something always goes wrong. It's too dark to see, but I can feel the space between our naked bodies getting wider and wider until Ben is beside me instead of above. I hear his voice rise up out of the darkness and I know, both instinctively and from experience, that it will shake with the timbre of an identity crisis. "I think I have a pornography addiction."

. . . . .

In the moonlight from the window, I can see Dave's face above mine as I lie back in my bed and take off my clothes. His strong jaw, his masculine nose. His eyes full of tears. I'm not surprised this time; I know what comes next. The whispered confession of a brand-new secret, the warm, sinking feeling of taking a young man's body deep into my arms, the gentle stroking of his hair and the assurance that, as always, "It's okay. It will be okay."

· · ● · ·

I am the girl who will take your secrets deep inside her vodka-soaked heart at two or three in the morning and in the bright light of the next day, I know I will never see you again. I will turn on the water in the shower so hot that my skin flushes red all over and I will cry where I can't be heard. I will get back into bed and roll the blankets and pillows up against my back so it feels almost as if there is someone lying there beside me, holding me in his arms. I can almost feel his slow, quiet breath against my neck even though I can only imagine the feeling. I wonder how it's possible to miss something I've never had.

Standing on the edge of that construction site, I smash every single plate. One by one.

· · ● · ·

It would be a cop-out to say I spent the first quarter of my life desperately chasing love because my parents divorced when I was little. And it makes me cringe to write that, for years, I wanted a boyfriend more than anything else. But, to be honest, aren't we all looking for love?

Let's face it: as early as I can remember, I wanted to be done with dating. Done with boys and bars and checking my messages every three minutes to see if *he'd* texted.

At five years old, I put on my mother's white silk slip, long enough to touch my ankles, and hung a piece of white tulle off my short curly hair. Then I grew up and realized I'm a feminist. A girl-power enthusiast lucky enough to have been born in 1990. I'm not sure I would have known enough to use a word like "feminism" at

a young age, but nothing helps you understand female empowerment quite like growing up with a single mother. By my teen years,
it no longer seemed appropriate to admit, even to myself, that
being someone's girlfriend was one of my most cherished goals.

Luckily for me, it was a goal that appeared easy enough to
accomplish naturally, in time, without requiring too much effort
on my part.

Growing up, I took it for granted that I would get good grades,
go to university, and probably break a few hearts. Those were inevitable truths, because they came from the lips of adults, and because
history dictated I should follow in my mother's footsteps.

My mother is beautiful. Right down to her core. She appears
to leap out of photographs, tall and slim, with miles of raven-black
hair and piercing blue eyes. In one family photo from the 1970s,
my young mother sits with one leg draped casually over the other.
With an unnatural confidence for a teenager, she looks like she
belongs in the pages of *Vogue Paris*, not in the rec room of a suburban Toronto home.

I didn't look anything like my mother growing up, but I listened to her stories about learning to drive with her high school
boyfriend and singing backup for her first husband back when all
he played were small nightclubs in Europe, and I believed something similar would one day happen for me. All I had to do was
figure out how to be beautiful. Inside and out.

For the first twenty-one years of my life, I pursued love and
beauty as aggressively as I pursued academic excellence and some
kind of undefined creative career. Like many young women, I had
somehow gotten the message that intelligence, independence, creativity, physical attractiveness, and a willingness to run with the
boys would inevitably lead to the fun privileges of sex and, eventually, to the ultimate goal: love. Finding a boyfriend, having sex,
falling in love … it was all supposed to be simple.

Until that evening, looking out over the construction site with a stack of plates in my hand, when I realized I'd been lied to. Every adult woman I knew, every magazine I'd read, even feminism itself had told me, in one way or another, that having sex was easy. Even too easy.

Everywhere I turn, I run into a baby boomer parent wringing her hands in shock and fear over hookup culture and phone apps that let you order a date like you order takeout. I remember all too well the shame of being a twenty-one-year-old virgin in a world that seems to value sexual savvy above all else.

Years later, I realized I wasn't alone. Millennials, the alleged trailblazers of the hookup generation, are actually having way less sex than most people think. In fact, as a group, we boast over 50 percent more virgins in the twenty-to-twenty-four age bracket than our hand-wringing boomer parents did when they were that age.[1] So, what gives?

As I watched those plates shatter on the concrete below me, I tried to figure out where exactly I'd gone wrong. I thought I had followed the social script perfectly. The trouble was that I had been prepared for a world that didn't exist. Everything I had been taught about sex and dating was a myth. And, as a bonus, I discovered I was woefully unprepared for reality.

As I fought my way ever more aggressively toward love — and sex — I slowly discovered all the little lies our generation has been told. The good news is, when you uncover a lie, you also uncover the truth.

CHAPTER 1

I AM EIGHTEEN YEARS OLD and I have never been kissed. It's my biggest and most shameful secret but that's not why I am crying right now. I'm wiping tears off my cheeks and trying not to think about my mother's big green minivan speeding down the highway, away from my dorm room and back toward my little hometown. I unzip the first of my many suitcases and begin to unpack my fall sweaters, my low-rise jeans, and my overpriced eyeshadows.

Reaching my hand down in between the soft layers of folded fabric, I feel something unexpectedly hard and square. Pushing my clothes away, I see an all-too-familiar hot pink cardboard box.

"Oh, Jesus, Mom," I say out loud as if she were still sitting in the room next to mine. "Seriously?"

I sit down on my unmade bed and stare at the bright little box with the words HER PLEASURE ULTRA RIBBED emblazoned on the front in bold, gold letters.

Of course. Mom would *buy me the most feminist condoms she could get her hands on.*

I stare at the box, and feel like it's judging me.

I've never been a fan of pink.

I root around through my piles of luggage until I find the welcome pack from my college. It's a big laundry bag filled with dental dams and granola bars, so I throw the box of condoms in there where it seems to belong. The good news is that I'm no longer crying. Instead, I'm remembering a walk my mom and I took along the beach just two weeks before.

In an uncharacteristic splurge, my mother had flown my younger brother and me out to the Atlantic coast for one last holiday before I went away to university. We spent the days swimming in the ocean and driving the winding Nova Scotia highways, singing "Daydream Believer" as loud as we could. At night, we went out for lobster and curled up in shared rooms like we'd done years ago. One night, as my brother lay reading comic books by the lamplight in his bed, and my mother and I were tucked up in our own across the room, I asked her to tell me a bedtime story. I was struck by the sudden realization that these were my last moments of childhood and I wanted to do something to capture them, to feel that feeling of being safe and cared for before going out into the world on my own.

My mother told me the life story of Virginia Woolf. A biography filled with loss, death, mental illness, and suicide. Her subconscious message seemed clear.

It was time to grow up.

The next day, we went to the beach. While my brother busied himself with sticks and tidal pools, my mom and I took a walk along the water, holding our sandals in our hands and letting the cool, salty ocean brush up against our toes as the waves breathed in between them.

"I've been wanting to talk to you," my mother said. "Before you go away to school."

"Mm-hmm," I said, already dreading what she would say with the instinctual teenage knowledge that a parent is about to do or say something embarrassing.

"You're going off to university and there are going to be lots of guys there … guys who are older and more experienced than you are —"

"Mom —" I said, trying to cut her off. I didn't need to hear The Speech again. *Don't be pressured into anything. Don't drink anything you didn't see the bartender make herself. Keep twenty dollars in your wallet in case you need to call a cab.*

"— and I just want you to relax and have fun," she finished.

I blinked and stared out at the ocean, trying to think of what to say. Part of me was pleased that she thought I was responsible and mature enough not to need to hear The Speech again. The other part of me was shaken to realize that even my mother thought I was a repressed prude.

"I think you're the only mother in the world to give *that* as her parting wisdom before sending her eighteen-year-old daughter off to college in the big city."

My mom shrugged with the twinkle in her eye reserved for things she found particularly exciting. Sex. Small amounts of responsibly sourced marijuana. The combination of brandy, salted peanuts, and potato chips.

"And I'll buy you some condoms," she added.

Then I finally did roll my eyes.

"Mom, I'm perfectly capable of taking care of that myself," I said. Even back then, my opinion was that if you were too embarrassed to buy your own condoms at the drugstore, you were probably too immature to be having sex.

My mom always had a good sense of when to drop a subject, so she didn't say anything else for the rest of the trip. It wasn't until I was back home a week later and packing my things that I spotted the box of condoms inside one of the suitcases she'd gotten out of storage for me.

"Mom!" I said, marching into her studio. "I was serious. I can buy my own condoms." I placed them firmly down on her desk and went back to my packing. It wasn't until I was already on campus that I realized she must have somehow slipped the box in again at the last possible moment, hiding it under my sweaters.

Back in my dorm room, I wandered over to the window and looked out at the swarms of students playing getting-to-know-you games in the courtyard while I unpacked and organized. Maybe my mother was right. Maybe my romantic failures were tied to my overall inability to simply *relax and have fun.*

Relax and have fun.

It's harder than it sounds, particularly for those of us who are coming of age in the twenty-first century. They call us "millennials" and "digital babies." Repeated over and over again, it starts to sound like nothing more than boomer code for "maladjusted." But while it's easy to repeat the age-old lament that our parents "just don't get us," the truth is that so many of us don't have that blessed hippie ability to *relax and have fun.* More than ever before, we are crippled with anxiety, depression, and existential angst that lasts long beyond the mopey misunderstood teen years. When it comes to sex and romance, the surge in anxiety disorders among young people is often cited as a main explanation for why millennials are the first generation to have fewer sexual partners and lose their virginity later in life than their parents. It's a strange reversal in the tide of sexual liberation that prompts me to ask: what are we really afraid of?

It's not merely the usual risks of disease and parenthood that have paralyzed us. The real problem is much more insidious, much more complicated, and a whole lot harder to work around.

CHAPTER 2

I T BEGINS WITH A QUESTION: "Who do you want to be?"

Every choice we make from childhood, and every choice our parents make for us, goes toward answering that question. From the very first moments of consciousness, I am crafting, shaping, building, and nurturing my best self.

My mother believes in the power of shaping your life. She taught me to visualize my best self and to push through anything and everything in order to become the best possible daughter, friend, sister, lover, human. From an early age, I knew exactly what my best self would look like. In no particular order, she would be brave, intelligent, beautiful, desirable, independent, and cool. Pretty much everything every young woman wants to be when she's eleven, has frizzy hair, and reads too much.

My first real opportunity to shape myself came when I started grade six at a new school. New kids are always untapped wells of possibility and potential, and I wasn't the only new student that year to spark speculation among our future classmates about who we would be before we had even arrived.

"Everyone thought you were going to be a boy!" was the first thing one of my new classmates said to me. No one knew what to think of a new girl with a name like "Nellwyn." It didn't help that my brother and I were the only half-Jewish kids in a French-Catholic school and we didn't know the Lord's Prayer. My mom had mumbled something about her Catholic upbringing when they'd asked for our baptismal certificates upon enrolment, pretending she hadn't raised us to be critical-thinking agnostics. Luckily for us, francophone schools in Ontario are notoriously desperate for students and my French was flawless.

The French boys I knew were always overtly sexual, and this new school was no exception. They told the dirtiest jokes at the back of the school bus, and they all had this *look*. It was a look that told us they knew exactly what our parents whispered about. That look was like a dare. "Well, all the French girls are doing it." But what was *it*, exactly?

André had that look. He came to us from the alluring province of Quebec (known to us Franco-Ontarians as "the motherland"). He kind of looked like Eminem; I mostly remember a blond buzz cut on a scrawny white boy. Despite being my fellow new kid, he seemed to belong more than anyone, regardless of the difference in his accent. He had unnatural confidence for a boy who was only eleven. He would have fit in anywhere.

I, on the other hand, arrived at my new school feeling like I couldn't possibly have been more out of place. After a girl in a plaid dress pushed me in the schoolyard, I resigned myself to a lonely, friendless existence. But then there was André. The boy who stood next to me for our class picture and asked if I had instant messaging so we could talk outside school.

The internet was really starting to take off and instant messaging seemed to be the communication method of the future. We'd all been cautioned against the dangers of chatrooms and the predators who lurked there, but, as I told my mother, this was *different*. Although you could change your screen name, everyone logged in with their email address so you knew who you were talking to, and you could only communicate with your approved contact list. I got permission to download MSN Messenger on our family computer and I was born into the digital age. Every day after school, I would log on and stare at the list of names, waiting for the little grey man next to André's screen name to turn green. I was a twenty-first-century Gatsby, longing for the little green light that made my heart skip. I didn't particularly like him more than any of the other boys I knew, but I adored the attention he had started to give me. I spent countless hours carefully crafting my screen names so I could present the best possible version of myself to the world. Exactly the version I wanted everyone to see.

The ability to customize a screen name to your heart's content made the possibilities for preteen self-expression seemingly limitless, and it solved the nasty problem of actually having to talk to your crush in person. André and I would spend hours chatting online together only to avoid each other in school the next day. It took weeks of cyber-flirting (or what my eleven-year-old self guessed was flirting) before he finally got up the courage to address our fledgling romance in real life.

As was usual for me, I was reading a novel hidden under my desk, so I have no idea what the weather was like that day or what allegedly important bit of geometry or history we were supposed to have been learning. I think Harry Potter had just begun his fourth year at Hogwarts when I felt a soft thud against my shoe. It was a bright new tennis ball. I wasn't as surprised as you may think since all our chairs had tennis balls stuck on the bottom of the legs to keep them from grating against the floors, and occasionally a tennis ball would go missing. The holes cut in the sides made them the perfect place to hide secret notes to your friends and they were easy to roll across the classroom floor when our teacher had her back turned. I reached down quietly and held the scratchy ball in my lap under my desk. I poked a finger into the cross that had been sliced in the side. The little rubber points were sharper than I expected and the note inside didn't want to come out. I was afraid to rip it. I forgot to put a bookmark in my Harry Potter and lost my place. Finally, I got the note out. A little piece of lined paper torn from the bottom of a notebook.

It was written in French. We all spoke English whenever we could get away with it because we thought it was cooler, but André wasn't bilingual yet.

Veux-tu être ma blonde?

It was a very Québécois way of asking, "Do you want to be my girlfriend?" Underneath there were three boxes and the words "Check one: Yes. No. Maybe." I guess "Maybe" was the precursor to a generation who thinks there's nothing strange about publicly defining their relationship status on Facebook as "It's Complicated."

I thought I was too young to have a boyfriend. Weren't boyfriends for high school girls? Or at least for girls who had gotten their periods? I checked "Maybe" and rolled the tennis ball back across the classroom floor.

The next morning, I crawled into bed next to my mother, like the child I still was. The sunlight streamed in as I snuggled in under the feather duvet and told her there was a boy who wanted to be my boyfriend.

"Am I allowed to have a boyfriend?"

I curled in under her arm and rested my cheek against her old flannel pajamas. I couldn't see her face, but I could feel her smiling as she looked up into the big, empty ceiling.

She said yes and I could hear her smile getting wider. She was happy for me. My mother is in love with the idea of being in love. Even if you're only eleven years old.

· · ● · ·

I grew up quite sheltered, despite my ultra-liberal late-boomer parents who'd spent the 1980s making art in Vienna. In many ways, I was no different from your average bookish, small-town girl who dreams of growing up and doing something adventurous with her life. But from the moment I was born, I was an old soul. I'm not sure if I believe in reincarnation, but if it does exist, this is definitely not my first time around the racetrack.

"Quirky" was a word used often to describe me and I considered it a compliment, mentally subbing in the word "creative" or "unique" in place of the vague and sharp-edged "Q-word."

I'll admit I latched on to my fair share of "quirky" ideas as a child, most of which were likely inspired by something I'd read. At eight or nine years old, I told my mother I wanted to churn butter by hand for our household, because that's what Laura Ingalls Wilder did in her books. My mother, always willing to foster ingenuity and creativity, obliged and fashioned me a makeshift miniature churn out of an empty yoghurt tub and a popsicle stick.

I never really liked playing "house" like the other girls, but much preferred "library," a game I assumed I'd invented. Years later, I fulfilled my childhood fantasies when I got my first part-time job as a clerk in our local library.

I've always been very driven where my goals are concerned.

Like many children who grow up to be writers, I was shy with strangers, but by no means was I solitary. I had plenty of friends and my brothers to play with. And although she fostered my loves of reading, writing, drawing, and butter-churning, my mother also made sure I got plenty of healthy socialization.

When my parents divorced and my father moved to Toronto, my mother kept us in the home we knew, a low brick bungalow with a big back yard in Niagara-on-the-Lake. She decided it would be better for us to stay in our familiar little town surrounded by orchards and vineyards. It's the type of town where phone numbers differ by only a few digits and the farmers who run the roadside stands put aside the freshest ears of corn for the locals. And yet, unlike most small towns, this one has a higher than average population of people who read Shakespeare and Chekhov for pleasure. Later, after I'd grown up and moved to Toronto, my big-city friends reminisced about finding broken needles on the sidewalk and having sex at fifteen after trying cocaine for the first time. They thought I was from a fairy-tale world where I went berry-picking every summer and had regular conversations with woodland creatures. They weren't totally wrong.

Sheltered as I was, I didn't expect someone like André to come into my life so early on. By grade six, the more advanced girls in our class had started buying their first bras and stocking up on teen maxi pads, but these things weren't on my radar yet. They were still part of my fantasies of high school: a magical, far-off time when I would have perfect hair and a boyfriend who was cute, moderately popular, and liked to play the guitar or paint murals. But André was French, so he thought about dirty jokes and slow dancing. And he thought about me.

Having a boyfriend (and the possibility of having sex one day) was an idea connected to a girl I hadn't yet become. She wasn't necessarily the girl on the cover of magazines, but she definitely had straight hair. And breasts.

I still wore my Gap Kids T-shirts and sweaters against my bare skin, but we'd transitioned out of sneakers for school and instead our flared jeans grazed the tops of shiny black loafers that made us feel incredibly grown-up.

If I'm honest, I don't remember much about grade six. I think our teacher still put colourful pieces of poster board up on the walls as a place to hang our artwork. I know for sure our desks were still arranged in groups of four instead of the adult rows of solitary tables we would face in a few years' time. I don't remember learning anything. I read novels all day long and didn't even try to hide how bored I was. I displayed classic literature proudly on top of my schoolbooks. I may not have known what the word *orgasm* meant, but I was really good at reading.

What I *do* remember about grade six is that porn had just gone mainstream. The internet had officially blown up.

We weren't *watching* porn — not yet — but I remember the makeup. The lipstick of the new millennium was all shiny gloss. Pink. Sparkly. Eyeshadows were blue. Highlights were aggressive, bold, blond. French-tipped acrylic nails were everywhere. Christina Aguilera went "Dirrty," *Girls Gone Wild* went mainstream, and even though we didn't really know what pornography *was,* the aesthetic trickled all the way down to my small-town classroom. We had purses full of shiny pink lip gloss and blue mascara, and many of my friends would soon get their first chunky blond highlights.

The day after he asked me to be his girlfriend, André sent his best friend Luc over at recess for my official answer. André hovered by the shed in the corner of the schoolyard. I could see him watching us. The late November sun felt cold, but it still hadn't snowed in Niagara and the grass was pale green. I could feel my friends behind me staring, too. Was there any place outside a book that I could escape being watched? Not if I wanted to be someone's girlfriend. Not if I wanted to be a woman.

"Yes," I said, and Luc scampered across the schoolyard to tell his friend.

I had finally arrived. Not just as an accepted member of my new school, but as a real, grown-up woman.

Despite our new relationship status, André and I kept to opposite sides of the playground. This is the way things are done when you're eleven or twelve. The boys liked to hang out on the baseball diamond or behind the shed while the girls took turns on the swings and gossiped on the monkey bars. Luc was our messenger. The only person who dared cross the invisible line between us.

Even after I became André's girlfriend, nothing really changed. We didn't hang out together at school and the only thing different about our regular nightly conversations on MSN was that the fluttery feeling in my stomach had gotten stronger. In retrospect, I think the butterflies were due to anxiety more than anything else.

Being someone's girlfriend didn't bring me the unadulterated happiness I'd thought it would. Sure, I was happy to feel pretty and wanted and popular, but along with that came unexpected churnings in my stomach and palpitations in my chest. I wasn't sure what exactly I was afraid of, but I sure as hell was afraid of something.

I managed to avoid my nameless fears until the last day of school before the Christmas holidays. André and I met halfway between the shed and the swings, our new winter boots dusting through the powdery December snow. From his winter coat, André took out a little box wrapped in Christmas paper.

"Open it later," he whispered.

At home that night, I opened my present. Inside a dark navy box was a pair of crystal earrings and a matching heart-shaped necklace. Carefully folded on top was a love letter typed in Times New Roman 12-point font and printed on a scrap piece of printer paper. We had still barely spoken to each other; our entire relationship was dependent on the written word.

Merry Christmas.

I love you.

I'm always thinking of you.

There it was again: fear mixed so tightly with joy that they created an entirely new sensation. To be loved was everything I'd ever dreamed about, so why did it make me feel so nauseous? Why didn't I immediately put on André's heart-shaped necklace and wear it every day like a normal girl would?

I kept it tucked safely inside the box. *For special occasions*, I told myself. I put on the plain, round crystal earrings instead. That was easy.

To this day, I have trouble articulating why my first relationship arrived so closely entwined with anxiety. Was I afraid of getting my heart broken? Perhaps. But didn't you have to be in love for that to happen?

The only explanation I have now is that I didn't know how to be the person André saw when he looked at me. Being a girl who wore a heart-shaped necklace somehow didn't fit who I was at eleven years old. I liked the girl André's letter was written to, but I didn't really recognize her. I looked at myself and saw a girl with too many freckles and frizzy hair who liked to read too much. André made it possible for me to become someone else. Someone made instantly more beautiful in her own eyes, because a boy wanted her. But being that girl made my insides flip with anxiety. I didn't like feeling I owed anything to anybody. Not wearing the necklace was an act of independence.

Besides, I justified to myself, wouldn't it be dishonest to wear a heart given to me by a boy when I had no idea what love was supposed to feel like? I wore the earrings every day; that seemed like enough to show André I wanted to be his girlfriend. Sometimes after school, I would take out the necklace and the letter that came with it and look at them again, trying to feel whatever it was I thought I was supposed to feel. I didn't love my boyfriend, I didn't even have a schoolgirl crush, but there was no way I was going to give him up.

• • • •

The turn of the millennium brought us a new wave of feminism and a new form of sexual liberation. Being empowered, in control of your body, and sexually free from the constraints of the patriarchy often manifests itself in unexpected ways. Miley Cyrus "blurs lines" nearly naked at the VMAs, Amy Schumer calls herself a "cum Dumpster," and millions of young women fall victim to the patriarchy's sleight of hand as these modern-day feminist icons reinforce hyper-sexualized representations of femininity under the guise of "empowerment."

My friends and I are the daughters of women who remember feminist separatist movements and bra burnings. My mother warned me over and over about the health risks of wearing bras with underwire and the moral duplicitousness of push-up padding. Anything other than a single sweep of mascara and a coat of lipstick meant you were hiding your natural beauty from the world.

In my mother's era, feminist debates went even further to question what was empowering and what was objectifying. The impact of sex work, BDSM, pornography, and even having sex with men at all was up for debate. Did choosing to be a stripper mean you were inherently a victim of patriarchal objectification of the female body or could it mean you were empowered and sexually liberated?

While my mother remembers second-wave feminism from personal experience, by the time I was coming of age at the turn of the millennium, the debate was over. The Feminists of the World (whoever they are) had decided that sexually explicit imagery wasn't inherently objectifying, given the right circumstances. They even took it a step further and decided that overt female sexuality can be a source of personal power. This is why you're more likely than ever to find a gender studies major dancing naked at a high-class club to help her pay for graduate school.

But, even though the debate has allegedly been settled, it is still far from simple.

When I was in my undergrad, I visited my most ardently feminist friend after she'd transferred to a new university a few hours away. A gender studies major, Stephanie was well on her way to becoming a self-described "professional feminist" and was considering a part-time job as an exotic dancer. We decided to visit her college town's only strip club on a Friday night so she could get a feel for her potential future profession.

Never having been to a strip club before, I wouldn't have known that this was a less-than-ideal place for our initial introduction. There was no burlesque glamour, no cut-glass chandeliers, or red velvet curtains; it felt more like a dirty sports bar than anything else.

The place was surprisingly empty for a weekend night, only two or three middle-aged men sat by themselves close to the stage. There were no bachelor parties or rowdy undergrads, just three men, a stripper, a waitress, and two junior feminists. Stephanie and I chose a table at the back of the bar where we could observe from a distance and use words like "patriarchy" and "intersectionality" without drawing attention to ourselves. We ordered a couple of domestic beers, ignoring a neon sign written in Sharpie advertising cheap shots with names we didn't recognize.

Steph and I talked about how good it must feel to own your body and be that comfortable in your skin. We talked about how liberating it seemed to really be in charge of your sexuality and not have to apologize for having breasts and full hips. But secretly I thought being a stripper sounded horrible.

I couldn't get my head around the way the woman on stage let the men reach up from their seats at her feet and run their hands across her naked body. Touching seemed to break a rule I'd understood about strip club etiquette, and that shattered any illusion I'd had that the woman on stage was in control of the situation. Perhaps she felt she was, and more power to her, but I could only imagine rough hands damp with beer snaking over my thighs and I had to look away. If it had been me on that stage, I'm not sure I could have refrained from kicking anyone who tried to touch me square in the face.

Stephanie called me a few weeks later and told me she'd decided to take a summer job as a camp counselor instead. I asked her what had changed her mind.

"It didn't really feel safe," she confessed. "I told my friend Kyle about the idea and he was supportive, but he said if I took the job he was going to come and walk me to and from work every day. He didn't want me leaving there alone late at night. I realized he was probably right, and there's no way I would ask him to do that for me all the time."

I wondered what was liberating and empowering about not being able to walk home from work without a male escort. I've never really related to the idea that exotic dancing or posing nude for your boyfriend is feminist act, but I can understand why other people do, and to each her own.

The power we feel we get from harnessing a sexual identity is about more than just having a satisfying sex life and making a feminist statement. It translates into all areas of our lives, becoming inherently linked to how we perceive ourselves. Overt displays of sexual liberation don't only signify empowerment, they also tell the world (and ourselves) that we are confident, self-actualized, desirable, beautiful, independent, and above all else: lovable.

I finally understand why I had been so desperate, ever since André put sex on my radar in grade six, to cultivate the perfect image of desirability. Even though, at eleven, that meant nothing more than being old enough to carry a purse from time to time.

So what does this image of idealized sexuality really look like? In my teens, it meant having a boyfriend with whom you had respectful, monogamous sex after you'd been dating at least six months. You were expected to be on the Pill and he was expected to wear a condom. It got more complicated in my early twenties. The girls I knew all operated under the same unspoken rules. Have sex with more than one or two people, but not more than fifteen or so. Watch porn, read Dan Savage, and be sexually adventurous, but don't go too far down the road into kink culture. Have sex with multiple partners regardless of gender or sexual orientation, but once you commit to a relationship, be monogamous. Sleep with whomever you want because you're a liberated feminist, but don't sleep with anyone on this arbitrary list of guys your roommate pinned up on the fridge.

This is the backdrop of millennial sexuality. We got so many of our ideas at such a young age from a vast variety of conflicting sources. At first, it was all whispers about the future and hoping a guy like André would simply be brave enough to hold my hand. Then, as the years went on, I accumulated more and more ideas about what I wanted my sexual expression to look like. I had impossibly strong convictions before I had any experience to back them up. I was a sponge, absorbing the examples set by my more experienced friends and the lessons I picked up from *Cosmopolitan*, Savage Love, and my sex-positive mother. The problem was that I didn't really know what any of it would mean when it came down to that critical moment. Would I be able to live up to my own image of the liberated, empowered woman I wanted to be?

I recently read a Netflix synopsis for an episode of the quirky ABC sitcom *Don't Trust the B---- in Apartment 23*: "Chloe encourages June to be sexually empowered and to dabble in some casual encounters." I want to highlight the link here, in nothing more than a simple TV synopsis, between sexual empowerment and casual encounters. Empowerment is so closely linked to being not just sexually active but sexually blasé, that it's become difficult to separate the two ideas. This connection between sex and empowerment is one of the ideas that perpetuates the image of hyper-sexualized millennials. In university, I was surrounded by women who were having empowering, intellectually fulfilling, feminist hookups regularly. It's that image which makes those of us who *aren't* having sex, those of us who feel nauseous when looking at a heart-shaped pendant, feel like we're defective in some way. It doesn't matter if you actually have feelings for the person you're sleeping with — or if you're eleven, the person you're dating — so long as you're sleeping with, or even flirting with, *somebody*. The fear is that if you aren't, you're not really empowered. You're constrained by a patriarchy that fears female sexuality. You're repressed.

You're a bad feminist.

But here's the rub: so much of that liberated, empowered sexual expression is still targeted at men. The naked pictures my friends took of themselves with their camera phones weren't like Polaroids kept privately in the back of their underwear drawers to look at years later with sweet remembrance. They were taken to be sent to men. Nine times out of ten, exotic dancers don't get naked for a room full of gender studies majors. They do it for men. While there are brilliant communities creating inclusive and empowering erotica that has nothing to do with fulfilling male fantasies, so much of the mainstream model of the eroticized female body is about the Male Gaze. And sadly for many young women like me, that mainstream model is all we see.

There it is, the uncomfortable truth: so much of our empowerment and liberation is still centred on men. We try to have sex *like a man*, instead of *like a woman*, idealizing and aspiring to the male model instead of creating our own. And what we often mistake for empowerment is, for many of us, drawn from the validation we get from acquiescing to the Male Gaze.

We all find our strength in different ways, and there are no hard and fast rules about what is "empowering" behaviour and what isn't; every woman will decide for herself. But overall, as a culture, we need to rethink how we've centralized men in the liberation of women.

• • • • •

At eleven, being someone's girlfriend was scary and overwhelming. I wanted all the benefits: I wanted to be considered beautiful, popular, successful, empowered, and desirable, but I was scared of what it might cost me.

What would I have to do? What would people say about me? No one else had a boyfriend yet.

I was beginning the same struggle every woman faces throughout our lives as love interests: what does my sexuality say about who I am?

I was safe behind my mother's computer. I could craft every sentence as carefully as I crafted my screen name. But this wasn't enough for André. He wanted us to spend more time together. I knew he did. He said so in his Christmas note.

André spent a good portion of our MSN conversations over the school holidays convincing me to go with him to a dance at the local YMCA in January. It would be our first real date together and the first date of my lifetime. The idea of being stuck in a public gym for hours surrounded by strangers was nauseating. But boyfriends expect you to spend time with them, and I quickly learned that they don't like it when their seemingly romantic proposals are met with hesitation.

My mother called his mother and established that there would be chaperones and other kids from our school. My best friend Justine was going and her older brother would be there to look out for us, so it was all settled. I wore an ankle-length jean skirt and a sparkly blue turtleneck. I thought I looked great. In reality I probably looked like a shiny novitiate. The nuns who taught choir at our Catholic school wore ankle-length jean skirts and turtlenecks, but I didn't make the connection back then. I didn't understand "sexy." I repeat: I was eleven.

My mother drove me into the city, dropped me off at the doors to the YMCA, and promised to be back in a couple hours. The gym was dark, so Justine and I hovered in a patch of light by the door. Music videos projected on the far wall shone over us, demanding exaltation. Little beads of sweat started to form on the edge of my turtleneck as I watched the older kids dance and waited for my so-called boyfriend.

That dance was a preview of all the parties I would ever attend. In some ways, they're all the same: the darkness, the music, that suffocating feeling. I learned quickly it's best to wear as little clothing as possible. Even if you're not looking to attract a dance partner, the key is really to avoid the heat rising from all those bodies so close together. How can a room so dark be so hot? The ceiling disappeared into the darkness, making me feel like I was at the bottom of a well.

Low-rise jeans had just come in. The butt of the early 2000s was a round, apple bottom. The teenage boys at the YMCA seemed to like it. Not one girl was dancing without a guy's hands roaming over her jeans. Chaperones not much older than the dancers circled the floor. They grabbed the boys by the wrists and moved their hands up six inches to the girls' waists.

At some point, they brought out stacks of pizza boxes and served up slices on brown paper towels for a dollar. I loved the smell of pizza so hot and so fresh that the cheese slides off, leaving a trail of tomato sauce and melted mozzarella in the box. Justine asked if I was hungry, but I didn't want to eat. I thought André might want to kiss me. First kisses shouldn't taste like pepperoni.

I kept checking the clock on the wall. I may have been among the last generation of women to stand around waiting for a guy without sending an angry text message. We didn't have cellphones yet.

I'm not sure how long I waited, but it felt like hours before I saw Luc come in the front door with André lingering behind him.

I smiled, but they couldn't see me standing in the dark crowd. I watched Luc make his way toward the gym while André hovered in the foyer between the two sets of doors. He walked in circles around the little entryway. He didn't come in.

I hung back inside the gym and waited. It wasn't long before Luc found me. He was alone; I guessed André was still pacing around the foyer, refusing to pay the entrance fee to come inside. Luc had treated his hair to an extra coat of gel that evening so it stood straight up out of his head. I remember him wearing a green sports jersey but I don't know if that's true ... it's the type of thing a guy like him would have worn to a dance at the YMCA.

"Hi," I said.

"Hey. I have to talk to you."

"Okay." There was a knot in my throat. I was glad I hadn't eaten any pizza.

"André wanted me to tell you," Luc's eyes darted briefly sideways before snapping back quickly. "He's not coming."

"Okay!" It came out sounding so upbeat and chipper. Luc obviously hadn't caught me spying on them; he didn't know I'd seen André. Were they hoping I would leave so André could come into the party without having to face me?

"Do you know what I mean?" Luc looked a little surprised, as if I wasn't quite as smart as I pretended to be.

"Yup, I know exactly what you mean."

I'm okay. I'm fine. I don't care.

I blinked back tears he couldn't see in the dark.

It was that simple.

I peeked back outside the gym into the foyer, but André had disappeared. I didn't know whether he'd gone home or was hiding somewhere inside the crowded gym, waiting to reunite with Luc. I wondered why he'd bothered to come at all.

I spent the rest of the evening crying in the corner, waiting for my mom to pick me up at the scheduled time. It wasn't love. It wasn't lust. It was sheer shame and humiliation. Suddenly I missed the relationship I had never really had and hadn't truly wanted.

The rest of elementary school passed uneventfully in terms of romantic liaisons. There was a brief drama when, the next year, André picked a rose out of some suburban garden and gave it to Justine right in front of me. We were all out trick-or-treating in a big group and he must have decided a rose was a more romantic gesture than a note stuffed inside a tennis ball. It was the first time I had ever felt second-rate, but it certainly wouldn't be the last.

I didn't love him. I didn't even have a real, true crush. But I had gotten a taste of what it felt like to be wanted, to be desired, to be validated by a man, and I wanted more. I was ruined. I could no longer feel as good about myself as he had made me feel. I had lost the beautiful confidence of childhood. It would be many, many years before I would be able to walk past a mirror without looking at my reflection.

The belief that I wasn't beautiful sunk into my body like a ball of lead in my stomach. I spent the next two years before high school trying unsuccessfully to wrestle my appearance into something I found more satisfying. In the middle of all this, I was gifted glasses and braces, and most of the boys in my grade, including André, transferred to a bigger school. With only three guys left in our class, and none of them particularly interesting, my friends and I were given two years to live in a precious, rare cocoon where dating was relegated to the future. We experimented with bangs and makeup to prepare ourselves for when we would leave our sheltered French-Catholic school bubble and join the mainstream education system. High school, where they would teach us how to put on condoms.

CHAPTER 3

I T WAS TIME FOR MY DREAMS of the girl I would be when I got older to come true. Somewhere in that big high school, there would be a boy for me. I would have long straight hair, I would be graceful. Unfortunately, high school doesn't automatically change who you are. Or your hairstyle.

Some people are lucky. Some people are born with straight hair and the natural ability to avoid walking into door frames. Justine was one of those people. She walked everywhere with her shoulders straight and never slouched unless it was over a drawing or a painting she was working on. She had that ability to make people happy just by entering a room and she already threw the best parties. On the first day at our new school, she was assigned a pretty blue locker in a quiet hallway next to a cute boy in our grade. I was sure they'd be dating within months.

I clutched my timetable with my own locker number printed at the top: 1503. I left Justine and struck out on my own through hoards of girls in Abercrombie sweaters and Ugg boots with straight blond hair pulled into perfectly messy buns on top of their heads. All around me were the sounds of friends reuniting, girls squealing, boys high-fiving. Lockers opened for the first time in months, magnetic mirrors were slapped inside their doors and brand-new backpacks were stuffed inside. I'm sure there were other freshmen with eyes darting every which way, but it seemed like I was the only one. Every time I walked past a bank of pretty blue or green lockers, I prayed one of them belonged to me. I wandered around the entire floor until I was forced to conclude that my locker was in the most dreaded hallway of all. I turned a corner and there it was: horrendously orange, opposite the gym, kitty-corner to the cafeteria, and right next to the school's busiest entrance.

Figures.

I learned quickly that I was never to have a moment's peace at my locker. It was like buying a house on the side of a freeway. It was constantly busy and loud with hundreds of people walking by, bumping into me, and tracking in dirt and mud so that when it rained or snowed I had to stand in pools of brown water just to get out my books. On top of it all, my locker door was bent in and I was always struggling to open and close it. It didn't help that all those hundreds of people walking by insisted on staring at me as I fought with the stupid metal door, trying desperately not to slip and fall in a sea of schoolyard sludge. I could feel myself blushing every time I needed a book or a new pen.

As a special bonus treat, our championship-winning football team had to warm up in the hallway *outside* the gym, instead of in the privacy of a designated athletic centre. Every day at 3:05 p.m., I walked through a double row of muscled, tights-wearing older boys as they flexed and lunged and stretched and stared. These were some of the most terrifying moments of my life.

One day not long into grade nine, I found a note graffitied on my locker. It was in pencil, so I suppose this was a mild-mannered vandal.

Hey grade nine beauty! it read.

I felt my heart kick-start into high gear as heat crept up my collar. I thanked god it had been written in pencil. It was faint and hard to read unless you stood right up close. I counted my blessings that, in all likelihood, very few people would have gotten close enough to my locker to read it. It was the most embarrassing thing to have happened to me in high school so far. Someone was making fun of me. That I knew for sure. No one thought I was a beauty. No one wanted to ask me out on a date. I knew I wasn't pretty. I knew whoever wrote that graffiti wasn't a secret, shy admirer.

I still had braces and the same glasses I'd picked out when I was twelve. I tried to buy nice clothes and wear a bit of makeup, but I never got the results I wanted. Sometimes I wore eyeshadow without mascara and wondered why my eyes reminded me of a washed-out rabbit. I waited until the football players all ran outside to the field, got out an eraser, and quickly erased the possibility that someone really liked me.

Now I question what had been so certain to me back then. Is it possible I was wrong about my vandal? I close my eyes and try to imagine how I would have felt had a boy asked me out on a date instead of scrawling on my locker. I don't think I would have reacted any differently. The knowledge that I wasn't pretty was too deeply and immovably ingrained. It meant anyone who thought otherwise was either a liar or had a shady ulterior motive.

On the school bus, not long after, I overheard a girl talking about her hair straightener. My mother never needed beauty products or hair tools, so I didn't know such a thing existed. As soon as I got home I walked to the only hair salon in town and they let me test a hair straightener on a strand of my brown frizz. It was like magic. I handed over my debit card and never looked back.

Then came the contact lenses and the merciful end of orthodontia.

My mother had remarried a few years before and my twenty-something stepsister was a professional model living in L.A. She embodied everything I wanted to be. Not just beautiful, but confident and generous and kind. It was hard to feel jealous or inferior around her because she was so lovely in every way. I hoped that maybe some of her sparkle would rub off on me if I paid close enough attention, and maybe, *just maybe*, I could be half as fabulous when I was her age. When she came to visit at Christmas, I found a brand-new set of makeup brushes under the tree and shyly asked her to teach me how to use them properly.

I started waking up early every morning to straighten my hair and do my makeup, and I read every beauty magazine I could get my hands on. I wasn't the only one who'd suddenly figured out the beauty industry; my friends were all along for the ride. We swapped magazines between classes and hung out at the mall sampling lip gloss and helping each other pick clothes from the coolest shops. We tried out new hair and makeup looks on each other and did photoshoots in our backyards to practise the poses Tyra Banks taught us every Wednesday night on *America's Next Top Model*. We went to the salon together on weekends to get our eyebrows shaped by professionals and treated ourselves to manicures whenever we had the extra cash.

By the start of grade ten, I'd found a new sense of confidence. My friends and I wore heels when most girls wore Uggs and we refused to wear anything with Abercrombie or Hollister emblazoned on the chest, opting for blouses and preppy sweaters instead. A few classmates even started asking me how I did my hair and what brand of lipstick I bought.

At the time, it seemed like with beauty came the boys. It wasn't long before all my girlfriends started going on dates, and soon my closest friends all had serious boyfriends. Looking back, I know the boys didn't pay attention because we'd suddenly mastered eyeliner; I'm sure it had more to do with them exiting their own insecure, awkward phases around the same time.

I came out of my shell right around the time I met Dan. Dan was in my grade ten drama class, but he was actually in the year ahead of us and couldn't fit the course into his timetable the year before. He and I ended up sitting in the same part of the auditorium each day, and it wasn't long before I developed my first real strong crush. Dan was tall, a little older, lived in my nearby town, and spoke French with the same Franco-Ontarian accent I have. He was dreamy and we already had so much in common. He was easy to talk to and I thought we got along incredibly well already. We hung out and chatted every day before class as we waited for the bell to ring. It was picture-perfect.

My friends all knew I liked him and Justine promised to bring me a cookie if I asked him out. It was a dare. So now I *had* to do it. To prove I wasn't a coward. To prove I lived in the twenty-first century. To prove I was as brave as any man. Besides — worst case scenario — at least I'd have a cookie.

I timed my exit after drama class one day so that Dan and I were leaving together. I walked with him to his locker and made small talk. I could hear the clock ticking away, counting down the minutes until the next bell. Finally, with a now-or-never feeling, I leaned against the wall, imagined I looked cool and relaxed, and asked him out on a date. What happened over the next three minutes is permanently burned into my memory. I remember the exact wording of the entire conversation.

"I was wondering if maybe you wanted to go to a movie sometime," I said.

"With who?" he asked.

This is when I had an aneurysm or a stroke or a short-circuit somewhere deep within my brain. I had no idea how to respond. *With who?* my brain screamed. *What do you mean with who? With ME.*

I had anticipated every possible response he could give. Except this. I never dreamed of this.

I don't know how long I stood there in shock. Finally, I managed to connect the wires between my brain and my vocal chords to choke: "I don't know ... with people."

With people? *What am I thinking?*

Probably that his answer could only be explained in one of two ways:

1. He is playing dumb to avoid actually having to turn me down.
2. He really has no idea what I'm talking about and is simply too dumb to function.

Either way, I knew in that second during my aneurysm that there was no way we were ever going on a date, and all I could do was try to exit the situation with as little embarrassment as possible.

"With people?" he said. "Yeah. I guess."

"Okay, great," I said before turning around and walking away. Neither of us ever brought it up again and our friendship, such as it was, completely dissolved. But the next day Justine brought me three Oreos. Over ten years later, that remains the one and only time I ever asked a guy out on a date. Because that day I internalized the screwed-up message that if a guy hasn't asked you out, it's probably because he doesn't want to date you.

．　．　●　．　．

October arrived that year with auburn light and pumpkin spice. The farms turned golden yellow with new hay and the pumpkin patches opened for visitors. I bundled myself under a new black peacoat and tucked my feet into my leather boots. I made sure my gloves matched my scarf. On a Saturday night, just before Halloween, someone's older brother drove us out to our favourite farm for their traditional pumpkin donuts and steaming cups of hot apple cider.

A bright harvest moon had already risen. The farm was clean and polished for its annual visitors. No animals in sight; this was a vegetable farm. Clean hay, dried corn, pumpkins, and spiced apples. Two by two my friends walked through the corn maze, holding hands. I wandered on my own, guessing which turns would lead me back out and which would only take me face to face with couples kissing in the dark spaces between the corn stalks. I wondered what my friends had done differently to get asked out on dates and find boyfriends. Didn't we shop at the same stores and wear the same makeup and style our hair nearly identically? What crucial step was I missing? What had they done that I hadn't? For the first time, I sensed the glimmer of a dangerous feeling. Maybe there was something wrong with *me*. Not with how I dressed or what I looked like, but with who I was in my immutable and imperfect core.

We piled into the back of a flatbed truck for the traditional hayride around and around the fields. Girls sat at the feet of their boyfriends so the boys could stroke their hair while the girls leaned against their shins. I sat on my own bale of hay and played with the ends of my long brown hair. Finally straight.

Being alone in a group of couples always made me feel like I was under an inescapable spotlight. No matter where I went, the light followed me. It made me glow with difference. With inadequacy.

You can't buy a pumpkin donut for one. They come in bags of four.

With all the examples around me, it was easy to believe that having a boyfriend, and having a sexual identity even if you weren't actually having sex, was essential to being fully and completely happy.

No one is happy after eating four pumpkin donuts.

CHAPTER 4

"OH MY GOD!" I said. "It's you!"

The evening summer sun made his hair shine. I leaned in to hug him.

"I can't believe you're here."

"Well, you wrote a play," he said. "I had to come."

I remembered why I'd liked him so much all those years ago, and forgot why I hadn't made any effort to stay in touch after high school. He had the same great smile, the same floppy haircut. He looked a little taller than I remembered, but it didn't seem like much else had changed.

Until he told me he'd become a Christian and had taken a purity pledge.

I had met Sam in my grade nine art class on the very first day of high school. I didn't notice him much at first, but he was the kind of guy who was good at everything. He could do math and physics, *and* draw and play the guitar. He had an indie-retro Beatles haircut before any of us knew what a hipster was.

It didn't take long for everyone who happened to sit in the front corner of our class to become friends. We goofed around in the art room after school, painted murals for the cafeteria, and planned for the day when we would be old enough to drive to Toronto and see a real concert. Sam was there for it all.

At the start of grade eleven, Sam and I spent every fall afternoon chatting in the school's sun-soaked parking lot, talking about art, and music, and politics, and all the things we thought we would accomplish when we finally grew up. He hung out with me every day. Just because.

And I thought he liked me.

We were sixteen and no one in our group of friends had had sex or touched a drink stronger than Coca-Cola.

When you hear about Snapchat and selfies and unsolicited dick pics being sent by fourteen-year-olds, it's easy to think that teenagers are all going to hell in a naked handbasket. But the truth is, even as young people become more and more sexualized, there is always a counterculture that receives far less attention on prime time. According to Statistics Canada, sex among teens is actually on the decline. Between 1996 and 1997, 47 percent of youth aged fifteen to nineteen said they had had sexual intercourse at least once, compared to 43 percent in 2005.[1] And, contrary to what you may think, their commitment to virginity is not always for religious reasons.

We need to rethink the distinct categories we've created in which we view the sexually experienced girl as empowered and in touch with her feelings as opposed to the inexperienced girl who is prudish, old-fashioned, and repressed. Choosing celibacy should not be automatically equated by the liberal-minded as a consequence of patriarchal, religious, or emotional repression.

In fact, researchers have discovered that a large number of teens are keen to abstain from sex for entirely personal reasons that have nothing to do with their relationships to these broader social value systems. At a program run in inner-city Philadelphia, health psychology professor Dr. Geoffrey Fong shifted the conversation about teenage sex away from religion and morality. Instead, his study focused on "showing youth how to talk their way out of that compromising, pressure-filled moment."[2] After teaching his grade six and seven students how to navigate their way out of uncomfortable sexual terrain, Dr. Fong and his colleagues followed up with the same group of teens two years later. The results of the study found that the students who participated in Fong's eight-hour course were "33 percent less likely to have had sex in the following two years."[3]

Popular culture is also rife with examples of this generation's desire to remain more chaste than their elders have been led to believe. Let's take a very brief look at one of the most popular young adult book and movie series of all time: the Twilight Saga.

Why is *Twilight* relevant here? Because its central relationship between teenage-girl Bella and immortal vampire Edward is built entirely on a foundation of pre-marital abstinence.

The crux of the story is this: Edward and Bella can't have sex because he will be unable to control his vampiric urges. He will surely kill her if allowed to lose even a fraction of control over his body. They wait until marriage to consummate their relationship. (I'm still not sure how the covenant of marriage makes him less likely to murder her in cold blood.)

How's that for a metaphor?

In 2010, scholars at the University of Missouri published a paper connecting the popularity of *Twilight* to the millennial romanticization of abstinence. Despite the popular notion that all teenagers are sex-hungry animals, the researchers found that it was the celibate nature of Edward and Bella's relationship that made the story so appealing to fans. "We were shocked by the interest in and praise for *Twilight*'s message of abstinence," they said. "We thought surely teens would find this message irrelevant and puritanical, especially against the backdrop of the hyper-sexualized American media landscape."

Although their research questions didn't focus on abstinence per se, participants in their study were eager to discuss the nature of *Twilight*'s central relationship and how they could apply it to their own lives.

> A fifteen-year-old girl reported on our survey that she felt "a draw towards a romantic and passion[ate] relationship that is safe like sex after marriage and takes things slow." Valerie, an eighteen-year-old girl, discussed in a focus group interview that she sees *Twilight*'s message about abstinence as one she could apply to her own life, "so I think it's kind of cool how it's like an interesting story and behind there's also something that you can actually learn. That you can follow in life."[4]

The truth is that there are plenty of teenagers out there who aren't thinking about having sex at all — or at least not seriously thinking about having it in the near future. Even after all those afternoons I spent with Sam, the idea we might have sex one day never crossed my mind. My friend Justine had been dating her boyfriend for two years already and it seemed perfectly normal that they were both still virgins.

Until I saw Justine and Sam passing notes in history class. And then I overheard them call each other by a special nickname. Maybe there was something missing from her relationship after all?

There it was, for the first time: jealousy. The kind of jealousy that makes you feel suddenly very capable of clawing out another woman's eyes. The kind of jealousy that makes you understand why a woman would wear an astronaut diaper to avoid pit stops on the drive to confront a romantic rival. I tried to focus on the

Peloponnesian War, but all I could think was *Are they more than just friends?*

Justine was beautiful, funny, and stylish, and I knew if she wanted Sam, she could have him. I would just be the friend he hung out with after school. To my teenage self, all other girls could have the guy they wanted just by batting their eyelashes. I had to struggle and pray and contemplate renting a billboard just to get a guy to think of me as something other than a friend. Since I had been publicly dumped by André almost five years earlier, no member of the opposite sex had shown the slightest interest in me.

The next Saturday, Justine and I painted oil landscapes on mini canvases in her parents' kitchen and I told her about my crush.

"That's so exciting," she said.

My oil paints weren't behaving themselves. Justine's landscape looked much nicer than mine and I was getting green all over my hands.

"You guys would make such a cute couple!"

I breathed a sigh of relief and all my fears melted away; Justine seemed completely genuine in her desire to see me and Sam get together. Still, nothing changed between us for months. I wrote angsty, romantically encrypted status updates on Facebook and Googled things like "how to flirt."

For some reason, that yielded no results.

By February, I was desperate. Our first formal dance was scheduled right around Valentine's Day and every one of my friends was bringing a date. I bemoaned my fate melodramatically to Justine during rehearsals for the school play. Perhaps sick of listening to me whine, she offered to talk to Sam for me, to try and figure out what he was thinking. There was clearly something between us, everyone could see it, and Justine thought she could speed things along. To a sixteen-year-old, this seemed like the perfect solution.

I could be honest and put myself out there without actually having to be honest or put myself anywhere.

I was hopeful, but I didn't buy a new dress for the dance. I had an old one that still fit and, though it wasn't brand-new, I was proud that I'd bought it in a trendy shop on Queen West in Toronto. None of the other girls had a dress from the big city and besides, my past experience with dances had taught me to avoid getting too invested in the idea of the guy actually showing up. Sam shelled out for his twenty-dollar ticket, but I still wasn't optimistic that we would go *together*.

Until Justine told me that he wanted to meet me after school on the day before the dance.

I don't remember much of our conversation; it is a still image in my memory. In it, Sam is looking away from me toward the school's main exit and the caption simply reads, "I just don't like you that way." I walked away and Justine, who was waiting for me nearby, looked up expectantly. I didn't cry. I didn't say anything. I just shook my head.

The next day, right before the dance, I dyed my hair a deep red-brown that shone plum-coloured in the light. I thought it made me look older and more daring than I felt. I stopped at Justine's house on the way to the party so our mothers could take pictures of us all together. Justine and her boyfriend posed in front of the fireplace with her hand on his chest. I posed alone in an armchair by the window and tried to smile in a way that didn't look lonely.

I spent the dance hugging the wall when the slow songs came on, staring into the empty space between the walls of the gym and the tight cluster of couples on the dance floor. Sam stood next to me, the only other person there without a date. I thought he might ask me to dance, just as old friends, but we stood in awkward silence until the song ended, and the next day we went back to being friends as if nothing had changed.

. . . . .

After the Valentine's Day formal I slipped into a mild depression. The reality hit me with full force: I was sixteen and had never been on a date or kissed a boy. Every time I thought someone was interested in me, I turned out to be nursing a delusion. I was the only single girl at any social gathering and the idea that anyone could find me interesting or attractive was ludicrous.

As I watched my friends succeed seemingly effortlessly in the worlds of sex, love, and dating, my confidence and my sense of self shrank more and more. Every time I had to go to a dance alone; every time I was the third, or fifth, or seventh wheel; every time I watched the other girls walk off hand in hand with their boyfriends, I felt a little more worthless. A little more undesirable, a little more like a failure.

I thought I was doing everything by the book. I wore the right clothes and I got the right haircuts. I went to the right parties and had the right friends. But no matter what I did, my best self was never good enough. Soon some of the girls at our school starting having sex for the first time, telling us about it in excited whispers.

I felt undesirable, lonely, and sexually frustrated.

With only one more year of high school to go, however, the end was in sight. I finally grew tired of my own melodrama and came to the conclusion there was no one for me in my school, or anywhere else in my hometown. I told myself if I could just get through one more year, I would be in university in a major metropolitan city and I would be immersed in theatre school with like-minded classmates. There, among the tens of thousands of university students and millions of urban citizens, there I would find the guy for me. This simply wasn't my time, and a year wasn't long to wait.

I decided to focus on being healthy, smart, and getting the best possible grades. I was chosen as a prefect and director of the school play, *The Wizard of Oz*, and I did it all while wearing high heels and waking up before sunrise to do my hair and makeup. There was no time at all for boys, but being successful still meant being beautiful, too. Who needs boys when you've got a bright future ahead of you?

· · ● · ·

"I found my wedding china," April said one afternoon out of the blue.

"What?"

"We were shopping in the States and I found the perfect china, so my dad bought it for my hope chest."

"Your *hope chest*?"

"What's a hope chest?" our friend Kaitlyn asked.

"You know, it's for when I get married. My parents gave me this chest a few years ago and we've been filling it slowly as we find things. My grandma sews me a tea towel every Christmas so they all go in there ..."

I tried to arrange my expression into a happy smile so I wouldn't look rude.

What if you don't get married?

"I mean," April continued, "I'm obviously going to get married one day, so if I've found the china I know I want, why wait?"

Then I remembered that the ring April wore on the third finger of her left hand had a Bible verse inscribed on the inside of the plain silver band.

"It all seems a bit ... *traditional* for me," I dared to say.

"Sure it is, but I like tradition. That's the point. Like sex," she continued, "I've always thought you're only supposed to have sex with one person. That's something you only share with your husband. It's not about religion so much, it's just ... how I think sex should be."

"See, I've always thought you *should* have sex with more than one person," I said. "But what do I know?"

It still strikes me as amazing that a seventeen-year-old girl can be so sure, in this century and in Canada, that she will be someone's wife one day. But it wasn't just the religious girls at our school who had adopted a more, shall we say, traditional attitude toward sex.

· · ● · ·

"Have you guys done it yet?"

Kaitlyn, Justine, and I were sitting in my mother's van outside Justine's house one evening. I was supposed to be dropping them off at home after a day at the mall or the movies or something, but suddenly the most interesting topic of all came up and we hunkered down in the leather seats.

"No, have you?"

"Not yet."

Everyone knew I was still single and had never had a boyfriend — or a date who didn't stand me up — so there was no reason for me to answer that question.

Justine and her boyfriend had been dating for over three years by now, and Kaitlyn had been dating our friend Sean for around six months. If you believe anything you read in magazines or see on TV about teenage romances, these four should have all been sexual experts by now.

"Why not?" I asked. I wondered if I would have that kind of patience. There was no way to know.

"It just seems too soon," Justine said.

"Yeah, it's too soon," Kaitlyn agreed.

"For sure, for you guys," Justine said. "You've only been dating six months!"

"I don't know ... if either of you wanted to," I said. "Six months or three years ... isn't that long enough to wait?"

"I guess ..." The other two looked at me hesitantly.

We three were among the most liberal, artsy, and feminist girls in our group of friends. None of us had ever been taken to church as children and we all dreamt of moving to a big city and living like the women on *Sex and the City*. But until then, we would be Good Girls. That was as much a part of our identity as anything else, and no one wanted to be called a slut.

But don't forget — the only thing as bad as being "too easy" is being "too prudish."

So how soon is too soon? When can a woman — or a teenage girl — reasonably expect to escape judgment for her personal sexual choices? I thought six months seemed long enough, a decent cut-off point, but clearly my friends thought otherwise. Who decides where the line falls? Is it the popular girls in school? Is it your best friends? Heaven forbid it actually be you.

I suppose I was lucky in a sense that I didn't have to worry about those things yet, but I didn't see it that way at the time. Tired of being consumed by my inadequacies, I threw all my energy into working on the school play in hope of distracting myself from love until graduation.

It was traditional for the art club at my school to create the scenery for the production, but that year the club had disbanded. It had been a fringe club made up of just my group of friends for a couple years now, and with university applications looming no one wanted to commit to six months of scenic painting. I tried not to cry and started calculating how long it would take me to paint ten different backdrops all by myself.

And then, of all people, Sam came to my rescue.

"I don't mind," he said. "I like to paint."

I breathed a sigh of relief, ordered the panelling for the backdrops, laid in a whole new order of paints, and Sam started sketching. I drove my mom's beat-up old van all around town to pick up supplies and, since I couldn't sew, I bought a jumbo pack of hot glue sticks and got to work gluing costumes together. Sam came to rehearsals every day and painted from 3:00 p.m. to 6:00 p.m. four days a week. No one ever came to help him. He would march in wearing his fedora, place his guitar next to the piano at the front, and paint and paint and paint. Once he'd made up his mind about something, he wasn't going to give up.

"You know he's in love with you, right?" Kaitlyn said to me one afternoon after we'd watched him pack up his art supplies.

"What? No he's not."

"He is. This is the Grand Gesture. He's doing all this for you."

"Trust me. He's not."

Kaitlyn smiled and shrugged like she knew more than I did, but she didn't know that Sam and I had already been down that road. Still, her words stuck with me. I watched him paint backdrop after backdrop all alone and I wondered if anyone in the world would do all what work for anything less than love. Or at least sex.

· · • · ·

"The guys are having a competition," Kaitlyn told me one morning as we waited for the bell to ring.

"Oh ..." I wasn't really interested.

"It's a competition to see who can go the longest without masturbating. Sean was out after the first night." She laughed.

Sam will win, I thought.

And I was right. Once he'd made up his mind about something, he didn't back down.

I should have known then that he wasn't the guy for me. I should have known that he would one day choose to be celibate. But part of Sam's appeal to me in high school was that, like me, he was part of the agnostic half of our circle of friends. He questioned and debated with the kids from more religious backgrounds, always coming down on the secular side of things and echoing many of my own opinions and understandings. But his progression into abstinence might not have had as much to do with religion as I would previously have thought. If you take a closer look at some of the abstinence groups that have sprung up on college campuses in the last decade, religion is not really always the biggest part of the discussion.

In fact, the main argument in favour of abstinence made by a Harvard University student organization, True Love Revolution, *appears* to be entirely scientific, though that could easily be put up for debate. Their website refers to oxytocin, a "powerful bonding hormone" released during birth and during sex which, in their words, is "designed to help married couples stay together permanently and trust each other."[5] Furthermore, they argue, these bonds can cause serious problems when formed outside the commitment of marriage, not only because they believe that oxytocin can muddle "the distinction between infatuation and lasting love," but because "when these relationships end, [non-married couples] often feel a palpable sense of loss, betrayed trust, and unwelcome memories. [...] There is no condom for the heart."[6]

Harvard student and vocal abstinence advocate Janie Fredell sees her commitment to abstinence as a form of feminism and a source of personal power. In an interview with the *New York Times*, Fredell said, "Virginity is extremely alluring [and its] mysterious allure ... is not rooted in an image of innocence and purity, but rather in the notion of strength. It takes a strong woman to be abstinent, and that's the sort of woman I want to be.... Everyone thinks we're trying to promote this idea of the meek little virgin female. I care deeply for women's rights."[7]

According to the *Times* article, Fredell views sex as another way men control women. "The more she studied and learned, the more Fredell came to realize that women suffer from having premarital sex, 'due to a cultural double standard which devalues women for their sexual pasts and glorifies men for theirs.... It's extremely countercultural,' she said, 'for a woman to assert control over her own body.'"

For Fredell, and perhaps for millions of other women who choose not to have sex, abstinence is a way of fostering inner strength and agency over one's body in a world where the female figure appears to have been made for public consumption. In fact, in my own life I know two heterosexual, sexually active, feminist, and atheist women who chose to commit to a year of celibacy. These women don't know one another but, five years apart, each decided that 365 sex-free days was the best way for them to achieve personal growth around relationships and a healthier approach to sex in the future.

The *New York Times* also made sure to get a man's opinion on the subject. Quotes by True Love Revolution co-president Leo Keliher showed me an unexpected interpretation of sex and masculinity.

Keliher told the *Times* reporter that, according to an abstinence speaker he'd heard, "the real meaning of masculinity is 'being able to deny yourself for the sake of the woman. To have that kind of self-control is really what it means to be a man.'"

For Keliher, the choice not to have sex or masturbate was linked to a moral code of masculinity and a philosophical belief in the importance of mind over matter.

I've always struggled with controlling my mind so, back in high school, I continued to distract myself from my failure to land a date by focusing on the school play. In the spring, the show finally opened and I was deliriously happy. *Look at this* thing *I made.* The glue-gunned costumes all held together, the microphones all worked properly, the backdrops were beautiful, and I felt like all my hard work had paid off. I started styling my hair in natural, curly tendrils and everyone told me I looked beautiful. There were only two more months left of high school and the rest of my life was just around the corner.

On the day the play closed, Sam came and found me in my usual spot in the hallway where I used to hang out and draw during my spare periods.

"What's up?" I asked.

"Can I talk to you?"

"Sure, sit down."

He looked like he didn't want to sit on the floor.

"Not here," he said, looking around.

I followed him to our school's least popular stairwell and stood in front of him as he leaned against the wall. In retrospect, maybe I shouldn't have stared him down quite so directly.

"I just wanted to thank you," he said. "Because I had such a good time working on *The Wizard of Oz*, and that's thanks to you."

I was wearing my red sweater with the deep V-neck. Half my hair was pinned back in a barrette, but I let the prettiest curls fall around my face. I felt my skin turn pink. I opened my mouth to speak, but he continued, "The only thing I wish" — he looked almost sheepish — "is that the Wizard would give me courage ... to ask you to prom."

My heart soared. I hadn't dreamt that *anyone* would ask me to the prom. I had finally accepted that, as long as I was still in high school, I would always be the girl without a boy.

"Yes," I said. "Yes, of course."

But his words from the year before kept echoing strongly every time I felt a little too happy.

I just don't like you that way.

I forced myself to assume he'd asked me to prom as a friend, but everyone in our circle adopted the same knowing smile whenever the subject came up.

I started to wonder if a friend needs courage to ask another friend to hang out. Or do you only need courage when you're hoping your friend will see you as something more?

You know he's in love with you, right?

I tried asking my friends. The girls giggled, the guys shrugged, and every single one of them smirked. Clearly Sam hadn't told them anything I didn't already know, but I could see it in their eyes: *Finally. It's about time.*

It was a few more weeks before I decided to bring it up.

"Do you get the feeling ... the feeling that all our friends are talking about us?" Sam and I were sitting on the hill overlooking the football field one afternoon.

"Uh ... I don't know," he said. "What do you mean?"

"I just get the feeling that everyone is talking about us. Our ... relationship. And I don't know ... I don't even know what it is."

I look at him sideways, he was staring at the goalposts. I turned my head and stared at them, too.

"I mean," I continued, "I know we're friends. And you wanted to be friends, but then you asked me to prom and I feel like everyone is saying it's a date ..."

He kept looking at the field. I began tearing up clumps of grass.

"And anyway, I guess I just wanted to know.... It's fine one way or the other, I just ... was curious ..."

Teenage girls talk too much, don't you think?

"Well ..." he hesitated. "Yeeeahh, I was thinking it would be a date."

I grinned.

"Okay, then, it's a date."

That meant it was finally time for a new dress.

I hated taffeta, crinolines, and anything candy-coloured, and I wouldn't have been caught dead in any of the usual prom shops at the mall. It was time for another trip to Toronto, where my very stylish aunt helped me chose an edgy asymmetrical cocktail dress that made me feel like a fashionista.

"What colour is your dress?" Sam asked me a few weeks before graduation.

"Black. Why?"

"Just curious."

"He wants to make sure his tie matches," Kaitlyn whispered.

Oh.

He must really like me.

· • ● • ·

My prom was perfect.

Until it was horrible.

I borrowed my mom's van for the evening and picked up the boutonnieres all the girls had ordered for our dates. Most people order rosebuds, but we were creative and unique and arty so we chose delicate orchids instead. Since Sam didn't drive, I picked him up, met his parents, and posed for pictures in front of their mantelpiece.

We all gathered at Justine's house with our parents for sparkling apple cider served in grown-up flutes and more photographs than I could stand. But this was the last time we'd all be together like this, so I smiled and smiled for the pictures and tried not to think about it.

The prom itself was astoundingly cliché and I think that's what made it perfect. I still have the awkwardly posed picture of me and Sam taken by the photographer at the hall. It's on a bookshelf at my parents' house next to my corsage of long-dead red roses. We ate, we danced, we sang "Sweet Caroline" at the top of our lungs. I skipped dessert because it featured kiwis and Sam was severely allergic to them. I'd heard horror stories about girls who'd sent their boyfriends to the ER after a kiss that tasted too much like a peanut butter sandwich.

For the first time in my life, I had someone to dance with when the slow songs came on. He wrapped his hands around my waist and our foreheads touched. We leaned against each other and smiled. Why did it take us so long to get here? Suddenly it didn't matter that we were graduating and moving away. We would have the whole summer together, and when I started university, I would finally be one of those cool, beautiful, popular girls who has a boyfriend at a neighbouring school.

I think most kids have their prom after-party in a house or a hotel, but this was the country, so we had ours in a field and everyone was invited. While the girls were at the salon that afternoon, the boys had all gone ahead to pitch our tents and set up two enormous bonfires.

By the time we'd changed out of our dresses and driven up to our campsite, the party was in full swing and the fires were roaring. I poured myself a vodka lemonade, but was careful not to drink too much. Sam didn't like drinking and, more important, he didn't like drunk people. I wasn't going to do anything that might spoil our evening. I was happy to skip the kiwis, but I wasn't going to say goodbye to high school without a little vodka. I sat on the grass and leaned against Sam's knees. He played with the ends of my long hair and rested his chin on the top of my head.

The field we partied in was nothing more than a long clearing in the woods dotted with tents and cars and our two big fires. The sky was clear and I could count the stars through the smoke. I mingled and tried to talk to everyone, even people who I'd always thought were too cool or too good-looking to hang out with me before. It turned out they were all really nice people.

As the night moved along, I tried to think of a way for me and Sam to be alone. My first kiss was so close I could almost taste it. Fresh and sweet and smelling faintly of soft woodsmoke from the bonfires. I looked up again at the countless multitude of stars floating above us. I turned to Sam.

"Do you want to go stargazing?" I asked him.

He turned away from me, no longer meeting my eyes.

"No," he said. That was it. The flattest and most final "no" I had ever heard. It was as if someone had flipped a switch or a timer had gone off signalling the end of us, whatever that was.

Sam walked away from me. For the rest of the night, he made sure he was on the opposite side of the party no matter where I was. Two, three, four in the morning slid by and we weren't in high school anymore. One by one couples split off from the crowd and tucked themselves into their cozy tents. Sam went to bed without a backwards glance at me. It was clear that this part of my life was officially over.

I looked up at the sky again and slid back the banged-up old door of my mother's van. I tipped the backseat down as far as it would go, locked myself in, and slept until the sun came up.

For years afterward, I wondered what had happened. What had I done this time to turn a guy off me so quickly? Was it because I'd taken that drink? Or did he never really like me? Did he just need someone to be his prom date?

And then there he was, in the front row of my playwriting debut, six years later. It was so good to see him. There's something about the kids I knew in high school, they seem to have a special place in my life that makes it possible for us to pick up where we left off and feel like the years between now and then have shrunk and shortened. After the show, he came out for martinis with the rest of my Toronto friends and secretly paid for everyone's drinks on his way out the door. We promised to stay in touch and of course we never did. But it always meant a lot to me that he'd come to see my play and seemed to take it for granted he would be there to support me at such an important milestone in my career.

Well, you wrote a play. I had to come.

Another three years later, I was facing a new milestone as I got closer and closer to finishing this book. I knew I needed to speak to Sam; it seemed essential. I was still haunted by what was unresolved between us, by the confusion about where we had gone wrong and why. Without a recent phone number and knowing he'd long ago deleted his Facebook account, I searched him up on Instagram, praying that he hadn't given up social media altogether.

There he was. A tiny number of followers and a short group of pictures from his work-related travels. I sent him a message and prayed that whatever had brought him to the front row of my play three years before had kept him invested enough in our shared history to answer.

It did. And as luck would have it, he was going to be in my area in just a few days. Even after all those years, the memory of my prom came back sharp and fresh. I was surprised to find that Sam was the only one of the boys from my past who could still spark a small pain in my chest. I think it's because he is the one who feels the most like a missed opportunity. I still believe we could have been good for each other, could have had a normal high school relationship, and maybe could even have saved each other from bigger heartaches later on.

On the morning we were to meet again, I woke up feeling seventeen years old. I felt like I had something to prove, and despite how far I'd come since high school, I wanted him to eat his heart out. Don't get me wrong, I didn't want him anymore, but I did want him to regret rejecting me.

I did my makeup more carefully than usual, and found some extra confidence after the friend I met for breakfast told me it was "on point." I really was seventeen again.

Sam must have seen me coming through the coffee shop window because when I walked in the door, he was already standing to greet me. We hugged and he pulled out my chair for me. He had just come from a job interview and was still wearing a brand-new button-down shirt. He wore his engineering ring on the pinky finger of his right hand and it seemed to me like a symbol, proof that he'd accomplished everything he'd set out to do when we were seventeen.

We talked about our jobs, graduate school, and who among our former classmates had just had their first babies. We looked up pictures of their newborns on Instagram and it felt like both nothing and everything had changed.

Finally, I asked him about God. I expected him to be as solid in his religious views as he was when I saw him at my play three years before. He was always a self-described "commitment slut." Once he set his mind to something, like abstinence or sobriety, he wasn't likely to relent.

"Yeah, I wouldn't call myself a Christian anymore," he said to my surprise. "I was, definitely, for about four or five years. But all that time, I felt like I was keeping my non-Christian side closeted. I was always trying to reconcile it with my belief in science and evolution."

I confessed that devout Christianity seemed out of character for the guy I knew in high school. The logical thinker, the lover of science, the believer in gay rights. He explained that he had fallen into a welcoming and fun-loving Christian community at university, and when I thought about it further, it did make sense that someone who was already pre-disposed to abstinence, sobriety, and philosophical rumination would feel comfortable in that type of group.

Sam also confessed that he is the type of person to overestimate risk.

"In high school, I could see my life so easily being ruined by alcohol or teenage pregnancy, so I decided not to drink or have sex."

He paused.

"I'm also just not a one-night-stand kind of guy."

Sam isn't the only millennial to be more risk-averse than expected. Just a few days after we spoke, I stumbled across a brand-new article on the homepage of Salon.com titled "Virgin America: Why Young Adults Are Having a Hard Time Getting Laid." According to 2013 statistics, the number of teens who'd lost their virginity had dropped by 14 percent for women and 22 percent for men in the past twenty-five years. Data collected by the dating service Match.com found that one in three twenty-somethings hadn't lost their virginity and 49 percent hadn't had sex in a year. As with most new studies, the numbers arrive before we figure out the factors behind them. Some studies show that the overabundance of choice and competition provided by dating services like Match and Tinder, combined with their lack of personal connection, make it difficult for some people to find partners. Often, many people who use these dating services find themselves making a lot of superficial connections, but few initial introductions translate into real-world dating as people are keen to continue exploring the seemingly endless opportunities provided by these online platforms. But this is not the only factor. Studies have also shown that millennials are generally more risk-averse than previous generations,[8] preferring to play it safe wherever they can.

Sam's progression into abstinence for religious reasons began to seem more natural. I asked him to explain his church's stance on celibacy from an inside perspective.

He told me that in his community sex was talked about with their pastor and youth group more than you might expect. (Although he admitted that men and women were always separated for those conversations.) I confessed, from my secular perspective, that a religious stance on abstinence had always seemed oppressive, unnatural, and often sexist. Sam told me that for him and his friends, it was exactly the opposite.

He said no one pretended sex isn't fun, valuable, and a very important part of a relationship. He also admitted no one pretends the temptation isn't real.

"But, like a lot of religion, it's about what they believe God intended. So yes, sex is there for a reason, but God intended it for a specific context: within a marriage."

Sam didn't elaborate, but I already knew that there is a distinction between people of faith who believe that sex is only intended for procreation, and those who understand it as an important part of a spousal relationship, emphasizing the power of sex to foster intimacy and closeness regardless of the reproductive outcome. From Sam's words, I was quite sure he fell within the latter group. In many religious circles where individuals abstain from sex before marriage, birth control is accepted and widely used within the context of a married relationship. For many people, restricting sex to marriage isn't about questions of children and procreation, but about what Sam described as upholding God's intended purpose for sex as an act between spouses. This distinction shows how there is room within religion to value sex for its own sake without emphasizing procreation as its only virtue.

According to Sam, sex isn't valued less, it's valued in a different way. It wasn't about repressing natural urges, oppressing female sexuality, or promoting heteronormativity; it was about valuing sex in a way they believed would lead to healthier marital relationships in the long run. Members of his circle thought stronger relationships are built if you come into a marriage without the baggage of sexual history.

"But sex in the context of marriage is extremely important," Sam said. "That's part of why, in a lot of churches, you have to go to counselling sessions before you get married. A married friend told me, like, three out of five sessions are about sex. They really encourage it within a marriage. And saying that Christians get married young just so they can have sex is like saying that secular people are only in secular relationships so they can get laid."

Sam also said something very interesting about masturbation. My free-loving upbringing taught me masturbation is an important part of developing and understanding your sexuality. My former Catholic mother always scorned the Church's condemnation of it as medieval sexual repression.

"We talked a lot about masturbation in our youth groups," Sam said. "To the point where I was thinking, *Come on, guys have other issues they might want to talk about,* but anyway, the pastors talked about it a *lot.* The way they put it was that fantasizing about someone and picturing them naked or in a sexual way is like taking something from them without their permission. It's involving them in your fantasies without their consent. And you're also taking something from their future spouse. I guess it kind of goes back to the commandment 'Thou shalt not covet.'"

I was intrigued by this interpretation which challenged many of my own stereotypes and preconceptions. Instead of repressing sexuality as "evil," which was the message my mother always remembered from her Catholic childhood, this emphasis on consent and not objectifying others was more progressive than I expected. While I'm still not convinced that totally abstaining from masturbation is either possible or healthy, I was beginning to see how some people could find their personal empowerment and liberation within a religious context.

With this burgeoning understanding, I was starting to get a better idea of what different expressions of liberated sexuality could look like. I thought of women like Janie Fredell, and began to better understand where she was coming from. It's a difficult paradox for many of us secular feminists to get our heads around, but it's important that, at the very least, we open our minds to the possibility of greater nuance in our understandings.

Ten years after high school and two years after he'd stopped identifying as a Christian, Sam drinks alcohol and dates around as he travels across the continent for his job. He now doesn't see himself being celibate until marriage, but he also doesn't see himself having anonymous hookups like many people who share his nomadic lifestyle.

The sun was starting to set and the ill-concealed seventeen-year-old girl inside me couldn't stay quiet any longer. She wanted to know, once and for all, what had happened on prom night.

So the twenty-six-year-old woman she lived in asked.

"I'm sorry. I was a piece of shit," Sam said.

I laughed.

"Don't say that, no you weren't." It wasn't that I wanted to let him off the hook; it was that I really understood how hard it is to be seventeen.

"I don't know quite how to explain it," Sam continued. "But I had this idea of what that night would look like and what it would mean. You know like when you're in the shower and you plan an argument you're going to have with someone so you imagine what they're going to say … and then you get to it in real life and it takes a completely different turn, and you're not prepared for it."

"Not really. From my perspective, the night was great and then all of a sudden you disappeared and everything had changed."

"I was overwhelmed," he confessed. "I'd never had to be accountable to anyone in my life before and suddenly I was accountable to you. And that freaked me out. I'm an introvert and I needed … what's the word for it? I needed to do that thing introverts do when they have to decompress. I needed to be alone."

"You could have just told me that," I said.

"I know," he admitted. "I was a piece of shit."

"No, you weren't," I repeated. "You were seventeen."

He laughed.

"Yeah, I would definitely do things differently now."

"Me too," I said.

"I didn't realize how badly I'd messed things up until that moment in my driveway the next morning when you dropped me off. We hugged and that's when I realized I'd ruined everything. But we were graduating and it was too late."

It's funny he brought up that moment. I'd forgotten, but that was the morning I closed the door on him and on my high school self. In the coffee shop with him, the day after prom came back to me in full force. I remembered going out for breakfast with the rest of our friends, driving back downtown from the campsite where we'd spent the night. Sam sat in the passenger seat and chose his usual favourite songs off my iPod. Exhausted, I choked my way through my eggs and tried not at look at him. Our friends pretended not to notice that he'd sat himself at the opposite end of the table from where I was. Finally, I drove him home and we stood together in his parents' driveway under the bright morning sun. I said goodbye and this time — for the first time — I really meant it.

At home, I closed the door to my bedroom and turned the music up loud. I sank to the floor with my back against the bed and held my knees to my chest. I turned away from the mirror where I could see myself in my T-shirt and jeans with my hair still curled and pinned in its professional updo, only a little flattened from sleeping in the car. And I cried over a boy for what I told myself would be the last time. This was it. I allowed myself the length of one sappy song to cry every tear I had left for Sam, for Dan, for André. Childhood was over and I was done. I didn't know how, but I was going to do things differently, I was going to *be* different.

Sitting there across from Sam in the Toronto coffee shop all those years later, I simply said, "You and I were never destined to be in the same place at the same time."

Sam nodded. He knew exactly what I meant.

CHAPTER 5

A S I STOOD LOOKING OUT my dorm window at the crowds of fellow college freshmen, I remembered the promise I had made to myself the morning after prom, and I knew that a crucial piece of my best self was still missing. Without a boyfriend or a date for Friday night, I could never be the woman I wanted to be, the woman I thought I *should* be. Not only could I never feel grown-up, I could never feel truly liberated or empowered. Without a sexual identity, so I subconsciously believed back then, I would always be repressed, a prude, a holdover from a much more sexist time. To be sexually free and empowered, I had to level the playing field and actively participate in tearing down the double standard. It was time to *have sex like a man*, and I had the condoms in my suitcase to prove it.

So there I was, unpacking my sweaters and books and feminist condoms in my first independent, adult home, and feeling completely lost. Like every other college freshman in the history of the universe, this was my chance to press the reset button on my best self.

Who did I want to be?

To start, I abandoned my unpacking and went to join in the Frosh Week fun; by the time those seven days were over, I'd decided.

And I made the wrong decision.

What I realize now is how much my visions of my best self were built around attracting and keeping the attention — and love — of men. My best self would be fearless because fearlessness is required to overcome that nauseous feeling I get in my stomach when I think about kissing a boy for the first time. I would be cool because guys are always more likely to date the Cool Girl. I would be beautiful and desirable because … well, need I say more? I would be independent and intelligent because that's what self-respecting feminist women have to be in order to reconcile our savage hunger for love with all the other fibres of ourselves.

By the end of Frosh Week, I'd made friends with the rest of the freshmen on my floor and, like most dorm friendships, we were a motley crew of misfits. Our group wouldn't last beyond the first semester, but, for the moment, it was enough that none of us had to be alone. Crowded into some dorm room or other covered with pop posters and pictures of best friends now scattered across the province, we got into sharing the stories of our first kisses. God knows how. This was pretty much my worst nightmare.

Here I was, one week into my new life and my deepest, darkest, most shameful secret was about to be exposed. I was about to be *seen*, so I knew I would have to lie. I couldn't bear the thought of admitting to anyone, let alone five near-strangers, that I had failed at one of the most crucial high school milestones. Never being kissed didn't only mean that I was a failure; it was evidence that my best self was a lie. I wasn't beautiful, smart, desirable, cool, empowered, or anything worthwhile. If I was, wouldn't I have been kissed?

I barely listened to anyone else's kissing stories as I started planning my invented history. It had to be believable; it couldn't be too close to a fairy tale or it would ring false. It couldn't have too many details or that would invite more questions. It had to be banal enough to make everyone lose interest quickly, but casually cool enough to prop up my desired identity.

It's kind of a boring story, I practised saying in my head. *I had a crush on this guy I was friends with and we used to hang out after school every day … and one day he just kissed me in the parking lot. It was cute. Nothing special, though.*

That was good, I thought. It was pretty close to the truth. There was a guy, we were friends, and we did hang out in the parking lot every day. I'd just leave out the fact that he never kissed me. Oh, and I'd leave out the part about prom and sleeping in my car.

Yes, that version will work.

You see, the best self is often on an imposing and unfair time constraint. I don't know exactly where the timetable comes from — probably some combination of the media and various cultural ideologies — but it's pretty much an unspoken understanding. I believed I had failed because I had missed my first kiss expiry date. It's like being twenty and still in high school. It's wrong, it makes people uncomfortable, and it tells the world that there is something seriously off about you, something fundamentally flawed.

I was granted a brief stay of execution when my new friends lost interest in the first-kiss game about halfway through everyone else's stories. I knew I'd gotten incredibly lucky, and that kind of luck doesn't usually come around twice in a row. If I wanted to keep following the social script, I had to get kissed *fast*. I could no longer afford to daydream about the near-perfect guy who would ask me to the movies and hold my hand. I couldn't afford to be honest with my true self, to be seen, to wait for a guy who made my stomach flutter. My only thought when it came to boys was now about how to achieve this goal. A goal in service of being the person I thought I should be, instead of the person I was. I had to ignore my gut and check off a long-overdue box in order to fit into my vision of myself and follow the social script.

And that's what led me to Henry.

Not long after Frosh Week, one of the girls on my floor invited us all to a house party in the student village just off campus where many of the upper-years lived. It felt very cool to be invited to a Village party just a few weeks into first year; this girl on my floor clearly had the right connections. Though I'd been to parties in houses before, it would be my first real *house party*, with a keg and people I didn't know who weren't all from the same small town. I didn't exactly know what to expect, but I was ready for just about anything to happen.

It was unusually cold that night, but I didn't want to bring a jacket and have to wear it in the house all evening or risk losing it. The walk to the party was less than ten minutes, and I definitely wouldn't be the first girl to grit her teeth and brave the cold on her way to a night out. Besides, the excitement of my new life and my new identity put a warmth in my chest.

Until we actually got to the party and discovered that it was an outdoor affair. The keg was set up in the backyard; no one was allowed in the house and the doors were locked.

Fuck. Fuck. Fuck.

Time to drink.

An older boy pumped the keg and poured me a beer in a stereotypical red plastic cup. It was good beer, cold and foamy on top the way I like it, but it did nothing to warm me. I crossed my arms over my chest and tried not to shiver visibly. I remember moving through different circles as my new friends did the same, weaving in and out, crossing paths, and trying to get to know the upper-years a little better. I was clutching my beer and clenching my teeth together tightly to keep them from chattering when one of the girls from my floor appeared behind me and tapped me on the shoulder. I turned, my eyes lighting up with recognition and my smile starting to curl, but before I could move or speak, she reached out toward me, pulled on the neck of my shirt, and poured her entire cup of beer down my chest.

I screamed, then laughed, afraid of making a scene when countless heads turned to look in our direction. If I had thought I was cold before, that was nothing to what I felt now.

"Oh my god," my new friend said. "I'm so sorry! I have no idea why I did that! I just thought it would be funny for some reason."

I laughed again and excused her, doing the socially expected thing by smoothing it over. I went over to the garden and tried to squeeze some of the excess beer out my clothes without taking them off. One of the hosts took pity on me and let me in the house briefly to dry off with a towel, but then I was back outside in my damp clothes and shivering more than ever before. I wanted to leave, but I couldn't walk home alone and had to wait for my friends to be ready to go.

I don't remember how I met Henry, but suddenly he was there. A boy with a blanket wrapped around his shoulders. He had a wide smile, dark hair, and tanned skin. I don't remember what we said to each other or how it happened, but it wasn't long before we were both wrapped up in the blanket, standing together in the backyard, taking turns wrapping our arms around each other to keep warm. We talked, we drank, we moved around the backyard together until we were in the alley between this house and the one next door.

I wish I could remember more about my first kiss. I know it was in the alley, away from the party. I know it was hungrier and damper than I expected. I know it made me feel like I'd done drugs and I didn't want that feeling to stop. But I don't remember how it happened, or what Henry really looked like, or even if I thought I liked him or not.

I remember the conflict. That feeling inside screaming that this wasn't me, this wasn't the way I wanted to do things. And yet, at the same time I was elated about having been kissed; it turned out to have been so easy to rewrite my history and erase the past. I saw how easy it was to be a different kind of girl, and I resented the idea that I needed to be different at all.

.   .   ●   .   .

No one ever changes overnight.

"I *never* do things like that!" I kept saying to my new friends on the walk home, afraid that they would think I was too easy. Waking up the next morning, I felt a strange mix of embarrassment and relief. I'd gotten my first kiss over with and I no longer felt the familiar crushing shame. At the same time, I had that uncomfortable feeling you get when you do something you know doesn't quite fit. Like when you try on a sweater that's not your style or sign up for ballet classes instead of kick-boxing. I should have paid more attention to that feeling, but instead I told myself that sometimes you just need a little time to get used to a new idea. I washed my beer-stained shirt and decided to move on, to see what else might be around the corner, to take things one party at a time.

Throughout first year, I tried to find a balance between my two selves, old and new. I went out, but not every weekend. I studied hard and I socialized, but, to be honest, I didn't stretch all that far from my high school self. Sure there was Henry and in February there was a very similar encounter with Ryan, a friend who was also a theatre major, but I never got used to that morning-after feeling. The Monday after I'd drunkenly made out with Ryan on the dance floor at a party, I made sure to keep my head down and my eyes on my book as he and his friends walked into class. I didn't want to face him, to see a drunker and messier me reflected back in his memory. I didn't have any regrets, but who I was at night was different from who I was during the day, and I couldn't reconcile the two.

Though I was very confused and didn't know how to handle my mixed feelings, I was starting to figure out how to *relax and have fun*, and I was more in tune with my peer group. As far as the social script and the timely coming-of-age milestones were concerned, I was back on track.

CHAPTER 6

THE FIRST TIME I got really drunk was at my mother's fiftieth birthday party the summer before I started university.

It was the perfect small-town summer day. The trees were dappled by the sun, the grass was freshly cut, and the lake was a calm, deep blue. Those are the idyllic country days I dream about and novelists spend hours trying to describe. The soft smoke from the barbecue; the deep Muskoka chairs; the condensation from a cold bottle of beer dripping out the corners of your mouth; the tall, blue-eyed country boy lounging in the backyard.

Tyler was an old childhood friend. He was always hanging around our house, sleeping over, and showing up for dinner unannounced. My family always greeted him with loud hellos, hugs, and a big plate of whatever was on the stove.

I thought he was lovely.

He was the kind of guy who could make you feel at home simply by smiling at you. Loved. Included. Special. None of it was forced. His smiles, his laughter, they were always the realest thing in the room.

The sun was setting and casting its soft glow over the day when my older brother brought out a bottle of vodka. He and his friends stood around the kitchen counter lining up shot glasses in a row. The real adults were all outside paying no attention, but they wouldn't have cared even if they knew.

My brother counted the shot glasses on the counter. "Nell, you want one?"

"Sure."

The word came out of my mouth before I'd even had a chance to think. I'd drunk a little bit of vodka before, mixed with juice, so I honestly didn't think anything would happen after just one shot.

Turns out I was wrong. And turns out he'd poured me a double.

My brother handed me a glass of orange juice.

"You'll want this after," he said.

I raised my shot glass to the ceiling and clutched the juice in my left hand.

I slammed my vodka down like a pro and drank my juice like a good girl. Almost instantly I stumbled back into the fridge.

"You okay?" my brother asked with a smile.

I stood up a little straighter.

"Never better."

I felt taller. My breasts felt bigger. Without looking in the mirror, I could just *feel* that my hair and makeup were flawless. I licked my lips and looked up at Tyler through heavy eyelids. I wanted to throw my arms around his neck and press my lips against his.

But he was on the phone. Talking to his new girlfriend, my brother told me.

After the party, I went up to my room and scrawled pages in my diary about how I felt. Not so much about Tyler, but about how drinking gave me a confidence I wasn't familiar with. I saw how easy it would be to turn to vodka to feel that way again, and it was clear that I had to be careful.

Not long after that night, Tyler went back to college and I went off to my big city university where, as we already know, I experimented with my new friend alcohol. I chased the false confidence it gave me, but at the same time, I developed a quiet set of personal rules about where and how I would draw the line. By the time I came back home for the summer after first year, I felt I had attained another new level of confidence and sophistication thanks to the shallow validation I had received from Henry and Ryan.

Tyler was there waiting for me when I drove back into my parents' driveway; he was in town visiting his family from his own college life an hour away.

I decided I wanted him and, this time, I was going to have him.

He'd broken up with his girlfriend and I saw my chance. Never before had I been able to land a guy I really liked, but there was no way I was going to give up. I didn't know exactly when or how I finally learned how to do it, but I caught myself *flirting*. I wasn't even really trying, but somehow everything I said and did seemed to say, "I want you."

In a subtle, classy way of course.

We drank more vodka and went on long walks around the town together at night. I criss-crossed my feet as we strolled down the middle of the empty road so that I stumbled a little and had an excuse to lean into him slightly. I pretended I was tired so I could rest my head gently on his shoulder. I caught him looking at me a little differently.

On his next visit back home, he came by our house in the afternoon. I was sitting at the desk in my bedroom, looking out the front window into my parents' garden. I saw his car drive down the narrow little street and turn into our wide driveway. I could see his hair shining through the windshield. I swallowed hard as if my saliva would push my heart back down my throat and into my chest where it belonged. I stared at him out the window, longing, uncertain, completely sheltered despite the belief that I was all grown up. As Tyler got out of the car, I saw something colourful in his hand. A flash of yellow. A rose.

He looked up and caught my eye from the ground. He pointed at the flower, smiled, and pointed at me. I pretended to look surprised, even a little confused. Demure was still my shtick.

I walked down the stairs slowly so that the ancient creaking staircase wouldn't give away my anticipation. Instead of meeting him at the door, I went into the kitchen to get myself a glass of water. As if I'd just happened to be there anyway.

"I saw this in the garden as I was leaving the house and I thought of you."

I still have that rose, dried and standing tall in a vase on the desk in my old bedroom at my parents' house. It was the first time a man brought me a flower, other than my prom corsage which I felt was merely an obligatory ritual. It was also the last time a man would bring me a flower for the next four years. I kept it because I wanted to remember that moment when he looked up at me from the driveway and I thought everything would be perfect.

That summer was the last time I believed romance was simple.

I'd moved to the city for university because I wanted something more. Living back home again, every summer night was the same. Tyler, my brother, and I would sit around the coffee table after my parents had gone to bed and roll a few joints. We drank bottles of Keith's out of a twenty-four case and did shots of Crown Royal from the three-litre bottle someone had won at the town's most recent stag and doe. Eventually, one of us would get bored so we'd haul ourselves off the couches and wander down to the lake. We always sat at the same picnic table on the right side of the park. My old fluffy grey cat would follow us down the road and sit in the middle of the table like a king while we smoked and drank and argued over how loudly my brother could play the music on his first-generation iPhone without disturbing the elderly neighbours.

Clearly, we weren't as rebellious as we thought we were. Across the water, the Toronto skyline rose up and shone to remind me of the new life I would return to when summer ended.

I lay back in the grass so I could find the few constellations I remembered my mother teaching me. The two dippers. Orion. Cassiopeia. The North Star.

The park had these wonderful hills we used to roll down as kids. Now they were perfect for lying back and looking at the stars. I listened to the boys laughing and joking and pretending to defeat each other in epic kung fu battles and imagined that this hill would be the perfect place to have sex. The grass smelled clean and fresh, the waves on the lake sounded calm and relaxing, the stars were romantic.

But what did I know?

I closed my eyes and imagined Tyler coming over to lie beside me. My brother and the cat disappeared in a cloud of marijuana smoke and he was counting the stars with me. I imagined him on top of me, brushing the little hairs from my forehead and kissing me, softly at first and then ... not so softly. I rolled over in the grass and asked my brother for another hit. I was getting carried away.

"It tastes like hot chocolate," I said.

That summer I made it my mission to run with the boys. I was lonely back in the country, my high school friends weren't around, but my brother and Tyler always were. I couldn't drink ten beers and go rollerblading like they did so I learned to shoot vodka neat with no chaser. It was my version of keeping up without getting alcohol poisoning. They taught me how to roll tight joints and smoke weed from a pipe. I stayed up late and did everything they did, but ultimately, I could never quite keep up.

They were big, tall, strong men who worked out *for fun*. I was strong only in my mind. Eventually, I had to give up and go to bed before anyone else was ready to call it a night.

I put it off, though, because once I went upstairs there was no turning back. After I took off my makeup and put on my glasses, I couldn't rejoin the fun if I decided I couldn't sleep. No one ever saw me without my Hot Girl Disguise.

I waited for the last of my high to wear itself out before I rolled myself up off the grass and walked back home alone. I went up to my room and had just put on my glasses when I heard a knock on my bedroom door. I panicked for a second and wondered if I had time to put my contact lenses back in before answering. I could hear my mother's voice in my head: "Men don't make passes at girls who wear glasses."

I decided there wasn't enough time. If I didn't answer right away, whoever it was might think I'd gone to sleep. Besides, I didn't actually *know* it was him at the door.

But of course it was.

He stood in the doorway just outside my bedroom with a semi-sheepish smile on his face. In another girl's life, he might have stepped right in and we would have landed on top of each other on the bed. But I look like I belong in a Jane Austen novel, so those types of things never happen to me.

I stared at Tyler standing in the hallway just outside the room where I'd dreamt all my romantic fantasies. He wasn't very much taller than me, but he felt so masculine and adult and strong. He was the perfect blue-eyed country boy in a plaid button-down.

I stared at him. I didn't say a word. The lights in my bedroom behind me seemed impossibly bright.

"I don't know how you feel about me," he said, "but I'm just going to take a chance."

He leaned in and kissed me gently.

I had never kissed anyone while sober before. It felt light and soft. Sweet. Simple. The opposite of the aggressive clamouring and clawing that came with alcohol.

I forgot to kiss him back.

My drunk self knew how to grab on to someone, run my hands through his hair, and make sure he knew how I felt about him. My sober self was simply shocked.

He had used the word "feel." This wasn't kissing a little at a party, this was about *feelings*.

I'd wanted a moment like this for so long, but I had forgotten to prepare for it.

He looked at me, waiting for my response.

I opened my mouth, but no sound came out. I looked away toward the wall. I felt my mouth open and close a few more times without making any noise. I wanted him more than I'd wanted anyone before and I was completely paralyzed.

"Don't say anything," he said before turning and walking away.

I fell into my bed alone and cursed the nineteenth-century author of my life who had made me this way.

.   .   ●   .   .

"I didn't think real people actually looked like those descriptions, you know, the innocent English rose."

"You're so sweet, do you even drink alcohol? I really want to get you drunk, it will be so hilarious!"

"You probably never swear."

"You look like you belong in one of those movies where you wake up singing and get dressed by little bird friends."

.   .   ●   .   .

The next week, my cousin Brooke came to visit from her own university town. Though she was only two years older, Brooke always seemed incredibly wise, full of advice about things like black eyeliner and push-up bras. Brooke was a big advocate of "Secret Sexy Days," a day when a girl wears her best lingerie under her regular clothes for no one but herself.

"Wait," she said when I told her about Tyler. "You didn't say *anything?*"

I nodded, unable to explain myself.

"Like, you were totally mute?" The disbelief was palpable.

"Yup."

"Okay ..." I could see her thinking, calculating the magnitude of damage I'd done to this potential relationship.

"I know," I said. "I know, I totally choked!"

"But you kissed him back at least."

We were walking down the middle of the road toward the lake, eating Timbits out of the carton. I dusted the sugar off my hands and fiddled with the buttons on my sundress.

"Nell ... ?"

"Not exactly," I confessed.

"WHAT?"

"I know!" I buried my face in my hands.

"The guy you've been crushing on for literally *years* finally kisses you and you don't respond *at all?*"

"I was really surprised." I tried to excuse myself.

"It's okay," Brooke said with confidence. "This can be fixed."

"You think so?"

"Yeah, I mean he obviously really likes you. And he's known you forever, so he won't just give up on you."

"I hope not."

I twirled the ends of my ponytail.

"Nellwyn ..." she continued, "how much do you actually like him?"

"A lot," I said firmly.

"Have you thought at all about ... you know ..."

"What?"

"About if you want to have sex with him," Brooke said. "If you're ready to have sex."

"Oh."

I hadn't expected that question.

I thought about it for the first time. Brooke waited patiently while I stared off into the distance. The first thing I pictured was my own body. The parts no one ever saw but me.

I realized I would have to shave, or get something waxed, or do whatever else it was sexually active women do. The thought of having sex for the first time was inherently associated with essential pre-sex grooming.

Like most millennial women, I am a unique cocktail of equal parts third-wave feminism, postmodernism, and ingrained patriarchal standards of beauty. This means that I know it probably makes me a bad feminist to get rid of 90 percent of my body hair, but that I won't stop until Kate Moss is on the cover of *Vogue* with a full bush poking out of her bikini.

The idea that I would have sex without some type of maintenance was inconceivable.

People today often blame our society's obsession with hairless women on the pornography industry. But I'd never seen porn or even flipped through a *Playboy* magazine. My friends and I weren't girls who ever saw each other naked, so where did I get this idea?

I turned to academia for some answers and found an article written by two scholars at the University of York titled "Gender and Body Hair: Constructing the Feminine Woman." Thanks to Merran Toerien and Sue Wilkinson, I was introduced to the story of St. Wilgefortis, a fourteenth-century saint the nuns at my Catholic school had for some reason neglected to mention.

According to legend, St. Wilgefortis, the daughter of a Portuguese king, had been promised in marriage by her father to the king of Sicily. Wilgefortis, however, had done what all good medieval women do when they want a shot at canonization, and had taken a vow of perpetual chastity. She prayed to God for help in resisting the marriage, and what did God do? The only logical thing that can be done when a woman seeks to resist the advances of a man: he gave her hair in unwanted places.

Wilgefortis was granted — by divine intervention no less — a hairy body and what I can only imagine was a pretty kick-ass beard.

Okay, so I've told a somewhat silly medieval story, but the point is that the associations between hairiness, unfemininity, and undesirability go back centuries. This isn't something new that has come about with sexual liberation, miniskirts, or mainstream pornography. The story of St. Wilgefortis really emphasized to me how ingrained some of our ideas about femininity really are, and therefore how much harder they are to reconcile with our feminist selves.

Women have desired hairlessness on the parts of the body visible to the public for centuries. Advertisements from the mid-1800s make it clear that any visible female hair, not on the head but on the neck, face, or arms, needs removal. When female fashions changed after the First World War and more of the body became visible to the public, the obvious response was to eliminate leg and underarm hair. Now that we run around in bikinis, the next "logical" step is to remove hair down there, as well. The long and short of it is for centuries women have prescribed to the idea that if it's going to be seen, it better be hairless.

Beliefs so deeply culturally ingrained are not going to vanish overnight. They might not even vanish over a couple of decades. Even though I know it's an illogical and a somewhat arbitrary social construction, I don't feel pretty unless certain parts of me are hair-free. And with all the serious problems in the world today, I'm not sure that's a battle I'm prepared to fight. It seems too much like a Sisyphean task. It's so much easier to get a wax.

Does that make me a bad feminist?

Probably.

How can I be a good feminist and still feel beautiful when how we conceptualize beauty is so often inherently sexist? It's only one of many ways in which I am deeply conflicted, and so I've often defaulted to whatever gives me the most confidence and makes me feel good about myself. When contemplating the possibility of my first real sexual experience, I made a mental note to call the salon and book myself in for their next available spot.

"Yeah," I told Brooke. "I think I am ready to have sex."

I'd never said that before, but in that moment I knew it was true. I was eighteen and I'd found someone I liked and trusted who seemed to have real feelings for me. It was time.

If I could get him to forget our terrible first kiss.

The next day I made two phone calls: one to the salon, and one to my doctor.

If there was one thing I learned from health class, my mother, and women's magazines it's this: go on the Pill *before* you start having sex. (If, of course, the Pill is your birth control method of choice.)

I knew it can take the body awhile to adjust to the hormone changes the Pill brings, and it might take weeks or even months before you find the exact estrogen cocktail that's right for you. Once I'd decided I was ready to have sex, I thought it wouldn't be too long before it happened. Whether things worked out with Tyler or not, I figured that there were plenty of twenty-something boys on my campus who might be interested in going out with me. I was determined to be adequately prepared when the time came. Even though I would obviously be using condoms, I wanted an additional birth control method in place, one with a higher success rate. What can I say? I'm a type-A personality.

In Canada in the 2000s, getting the Pill is easy. Especially if you are eighteen or older. According to my friends, all I had to do was go to my doctor and ask for it. I walked into her office with the confidence and maturity I knew I needed to make such an important adult decision. I sat on the examination bed with my legs dangling above the floor and tried not to crinkle the paper beneath me as I asked for the Pill.

"Do you have a boyfriend?" my doctor asked.

I was taken aback; I hadn't been expecting this question and I couldn't see how it was relevant.

What if I said "no"? Would she deny me the prescription?

I didn't think fast enough to lie with a simple "Yes, yes I do have a boyfriend. He's also a virgin and he's going to lay rose petals at my feet before deflowering me in the ultimate act of love and respect while smooth jazz plays softly in the background."

"Well, no, not really," I stammered. "But there's a guy and I think he might be my boyfriend … soon."

"Then why do you want the Pill now?" she asked me.

I inhaled sharply as my eyes widened even bigger than usual. I swallowed hard.

"Because I know it can take your body awhile to adjust and to find the right pill and I want to be prepared."

I didn't think that an adult woman who'd actually paid attention in health class and was making the responsible choice to be proactive about her reproductive health would be subject to those kinds of questions. Suddenly I felt like an irresponsible child. A bad girl.

But the doctor reached for her prescription pad.

Armed with my little pack of birth control pills and a fresh bikini wax, I was ready for sex.

• • ● • •

I think if Tyler had been any other guy, our disastrous first kiss would have put him off entirely. He probably wouldn't have called or come around again. My cute and agonizingly planned texts would have gotten short but courteous responses that eventually faded away.

But some people are meant to stay in your life forever; Tyler would always come back again. Even if he came by only to see my brothers, I knew I would get another chance with him.

On another summer night, he, my brother, and I sat drinking beers and doing shots at my parents' kitchen table yet again. I was eager to be alone with Tyler, but I knew that drinking too much beer will make anyone have to pee. I just had to wait out my brother's bladder, and it didn't take long.

Alone in the kitchen with Tyler, I moved toward the sink, opposite from where he sat in front of our empty shot glasses and half-drunk cans of lukewarm beer.

I knew from reading Jane Austen: "Your figures appear to the greatest advantage in walking."[1]

I walked across the kitchen and dusted my fingertips along the edge of the wood countertops. Everyone else was asleep. The room smelled of summer and a fresh bag of family-sized kettle-cooked potato chips. Original flavour. Salty.

I leaned back against the sink so my bare hipbones stuck out and my T-shirt inched up. I breathed in, directing the air to my chest so my breasts swelled.

"Jesus," he exhaled.

He walked across the room and put his hands on my hips.

"I want to kiss you," he said.

"Then, why haven't you?" This kind of confidence was completely new to me, and I didn't know where it came from. It was probably a combination of the drinking, the yellow rose, and the belief that he really did like me.

He bent his head down and ran his hands along my waist. I felt myself go weak in the knees. Was it the alcohol or was it him?

My whole body had turned to lava, hot and melting and threatening to spill all over my parents' kitchen floor.

"I feel like I'm melting," I mumbled.

He kissed me again.

I slid a little further down, but he caught me before my knees gave way.

"Jesus," he said again. "You really are melting."

I heard my brother's heavy footsteps leaping down the stairs two by two and we broke apart. We wouldn't find another moment alone for the rest of the weekend and on Sunday night he left town.

Later that week, my friend Stephanie came to visit with a bottle of vodka and a carton of pink lemonade. We took our cocktails down to the park by the lake where she perched on top of our picnic table and I sprawled in the grass on my usual hillside.

"I want him to know I like him," I said.

Apparently, I didn't think making out with him in my parents' kitchen was evidence enough.

"Nothing's happening," I complained. "I want things to move faster."

"You should send him a sexy text message." Stephanie said matter-of-factly. "Trust me. That always works."

"I can't do that! I don't even know what to say!"

"I'll write it for you."

I hesitated. This did seem like the perfect solution.

"Okay," I said, handing her my pink cellphone. "Just write a draft and don't send it until I read it."

"Of course not, don't worry."

I really trusted Stephanie.

Eight years later as I write this, Stephanie is a professional feminist with a healthy handful of degrees in gender studies. She is still the first person I go to for advice on anything to do with mainstream feminism, vibrators, et cetera.

"I feel like sexting has become the way to start a relationship," Stephanie said to me recently over Skype. "Not now, but I'm thinking when I was twenty-two, or twenty-three, it's the undergrad culture of 'casual sex might lead to more.' For me, I felt like I was participatory in sexualizing myself in order to try and gain a guy who would feel more than just a sexual connection. But I felt that was the route I had to go. Like 'why would a guy be interested if I'm not giving it up right away?' That was my fear. That if I don't appear sexy and cool, then why would he ever want to date me?"

Stephanie swept on some subtle eyeliner as we spoke while I sat on my sofa in sweatpants a hundred kilometres away.

"So showing that you are a sexual person," I said, "and having this crafted sexual identity that you've created by choosing the specific words that you're going to put in your text ..." I hesitated before reframing. "Building that identity is what you felt would make a guy interested in you — not only sexually, but down the road romantically. Is that right?"

"Yeah. Exactly."

Back in 2009, sexting was what we thought would make a guy interested, so we were all for it. After a few moments of typing, Stephanie handed me back my phone.

"There. That will get his attention. Guaranteed."

My stomach flipped. Stephanie wasn't messing around. This was seriously next-level stuff.

"*Oh my god!*" I squealed. "I can't send that!"

"Why not?"

I didn't know why not. Didn't I want to be sexy? Didn't I *really*, *really* like this guy? Didn't I want to lose my virginity?

Yes. Yes. Yes.

I drank some more vodka lemonade and pressed send before I could think twice.

Stephanie cheered as we raised our cups.

"Congratulations! Your first sext!" It was like a rite of passage.

After that, I thought I had succeeded in making Tyler see me as a sexual person. A Hot Girl. But the summer was drawing to a close and he still hadn't asked me out on a date. He texted me all the time.

Good Morning Beautiful.

How's your day going?

I had a dream about you last night.

I convinced myself it was because we lived too far apart. He was technically living in his university town that summer and we only saw him when he visited his parents on his days off. It wasn't practical for us to really date. But as soon as I went back to school, we would live only half an hour from each other. The last week of August arrived and I gave myself an ultimatum; I knew this would be the last time I would see him before I left for school.

We walked home together from the only bar in town. A long, long walk under the big old trees by the edge of the golf course. A long walk along the lake where we could see the glimmering lights of Toronto's downtown skyline rising up from the darkness across the water and following us home. We strolled up the middle of the street as we always did, the only people in sight. The cottages were all dark and sleeping like grandmothers wrapped in flowery blankets of late summer blooms.

"What's going to happen when I go back to school?" I asked.

I couldn't say what I wanted. I had to give him all the power.

"Yeah, I guess we won't see each other as much."

"Well, technically we'll be closer," I pointed out. "We could see each other more. If that's what we want."

He didn't say anything.

I kicked a stone along as we walked.

"I think you're really great," he said. "You know that."

We walked past the swamp and the smell of algae swimming in pools of warm summer water tickled my nose.

"I don't want to just sleep with you and have it not mean anything. I like you. You're a girlfriend kind of girl."

I barely had a second to feel the bliss I had been waiting for. The happiness I was sure would come with words like those.

"But I don't want a girlfriend right now," he said.

"So you won't sleep with me unless I'm your girlfriend, but you don't want a girlfriend."

"Yeah."

"Well, I guess that answers that."

There it was again: proof that my life was written by a nineteenth-century author. I was the good girl, the girl who read books and baked pies. The girl you don't necessarily want to be your girlfriend, but the girl who is, for some reason, deemed "too good" for casual sex.

What makes a person "too good" for hooking up?

Did I fail to prove I was exactly the right kind of sexy?

I knew I must have, but I also thought I'd done everything right.

I'd worn the low-rise jeans and the push-up bras. I'd drunk alcohol and smoked weed. I'd flirted and leaned in and tucked my elbows into my waist as I talked so that my breasts looked bigger. I sent dirty text messages.

I guessed I just hadn't done enough.

Looking back on that summer and talking about it with Tyler years later, I see two young people who didn't know how to handle their feelings. We thought we were adults but we still had so much to figure out about sex and relationships and being truly honest with each other. We were two people who overthought everything, and we had a lifelong friendship at stake. I was willing to risk it, he wasn't.

But at the time, all I heard, all I felt, was that I'd been Madonna-Whored. I felt like I was a victim of this sexist mentality in which men consciously or unconsciously distinguish between the women they desire and the women they respect. And that knowledge shaped a lot of what was about to come next in my life.

I resented Tyler's words as much as I obsessed over them. What puts women into one of those two categories: "girlfriend material" or "hookup material"? What is it that makes men decide you're the type of girl who couldn't possibly be interested in casual sex, and that even if you *are* interested, it's somehow beneath you?

I felt like I wasn't given a choice in how I wanted to express myself or my sexuality. Tyler had put me in a category, classified me as a type, and left no room for me to have any voice or agency or individual wants, needs, and desires. It was as though he thought he knew what was best for me, based on the category he himself had put me in.

I was angry, but I thought I was in love with him. And so my agony continued.

We kept texting and flirting and calling each other in the middle of the night from our two campuses in different Toronto suburbs. I counted down the days until Thanksgiving when we would both be home again and I would have another chance to change his mind about me. But then I found out, thanks to Facebook, that he had gotten himself a new girlfriend. I was completely crushed. In less than six weeks, the guy who didn't want a girlfriend had found someone else, someone who was worthier of him than me. For the first time since I could remember, he didn't come over on Thanksgiving for his extra slice of my mom's pumpkin pie.

Back at school, I moped about, finding more alcohol to drink and more boys to kiss. Tyler kept in touch, even at one point going so far as to ask me to help him make his girlfriend jealous. I told him to stop speaking to me.

I was done being the second-best girl.

Severing ties with Tyler helped me resolve to be even bolder, to put myself "out there" more, to become an "it" girl. *From now on*, I decided, *I'm going to go to all the right parties and flirt with all the right people.* I was determined to try to become the kind of girl who was *both* datable and fuckable.

CHAPTER 7

"I CONSIDER ALCOHOL WASTED if I don't make out with anyone."

I said this as a joke, but by then I was seriously deep into my party-girl phase and it was at least a little bit true.

We live in a culture that inherently associates happiness and freedom with sexual liberation and a satisfying sex life. The idealized definition of sexual liberation and satisfaction we have internalized is drawn from the examples we see, both in the mainstream media and among our social circles. I grew up reading *Cosmopolitan* and although, by the time I'd reached university, I'd had enough feminist education to know that its pages are full of shit, I'd still internalized its ideal of the "Fun Fearless Female." The *Cosmo* girl we'd read about when we were fourteen was the ideal "assertive, sexual, and attractive twenty-something female."[1] The

Psychologist Elizabeth L. Paul discusses this psychology of a "wanted self" and "unwanted self" in relation to campus culture and the popularity of hooking up in college. She confirms that "the desired identity promulgated in popular media is one of non-chalance about sex and easy sexual prowess."[2] But it isn't just the

Evil Media painting a sexualized picture of the "perfect" woman. Branches of feminism and the sexual liberation movement have also told women that expressing our sexuality is part of being independent and equal with men. The freedom to be openly sexual has become an important part of how many of us express our social and political liberation.

Paul attributes some of the need young women feel to craft a sexualized "wanted self" to the feminist movement: "Perhaps oxymoronically, both the power of the women's movement and the pervasiveness of sexuality in contemporary culture urge women to claim their sexuality, permitting women to desire a sexual self."[3] The postmodern feminist is liberated and equal partly because she is expressing her sexuality in a way previously prohibited for women, and she has smashed the sexual double standard by accepting and manifesting a shame-free sexual self.

The rightful and necessary quest for sexual equality has taken an interesting and somewhat questionable turn, however, by framing female sexuality in relation to traditional and stereotypical ideas of male sexuality. Somewhere along the way, the idea of a liberated and egalitarian female sexuality became less about the freedom of personal expression and more about having sex *like a man*. Instead of really investigating what different versions of a liberated sex life could look like for women, pop culture feminism has equated female liberation with a generalized masculine model. Do we all remember the *Sex and the City* pilot? Carrie Bradshaw's driving question, in part promoted by her friend Samantha, who quips about women having "the equal luxury to treat men like sex objects," is whether women can "have sex like a man" and "throttle up on power."[4] While equality, female empowerment, and the elimination of double standards are important feminist ideals we should all get behind, we may want to start thinking more critically about what *kind* of equality and empowerment we're being sold by this so-called feminist popular culture.

While I'm sure there are many women who relish the idea of "having sex like a man" and draw empowerment from it, it is a bit of a sexist notion to equate female sexual liberation so strongly with the idea of emulating men — and an outdated stereotype of men, no less. Furthermore, the idea that empowerment and liberation come from enacting this very specific type of sexuality leaves little room for divergence and creates a conflict between how the individual may differ from the popular ideology. Equating female empowerment and liberation with a specific kind of sexuality modelled on a stereotypical male example may be part of what has contributed to the rise of hookup culture, particularly on college campuses.

Back in my second year of university, I thought I knew a lot about feminism and the media influence on our culture, but I didn't really make the connection between how my "wanted self" was informed by this idealized woman I had internalized. I wanted to be Carrie Bradshaw from *Sex and the City* or a *Cosmo* girl. The postmodern feminist who is beautiful and smart, who has a great job and who is financially independent. Who drinks cocktails after work and whose casual hookups always end in mind-blowing orgasms thanks to her hyper-awareness of her own desires and needs.

That fall, some high-achieving students in third year formed an independent theatre company. They rented a gallery space on campus and announced that they were in pre-production for their inaugural show, *Closer*, some of which takes place in a strip club.

My friend Kristen was the production designer on the project, and she imagined the strip club scenes full of video projections with bright pink lights and lots of girls dancing anonymously in silhouette.

She asked me to play one of the girls.

"I just need to film you for, like, thirty minutes," she said. "And you'll be totally in silhouette so no one will even know it's you."

"Sure," I said. "It'll be fun."

This might have been when I started making life decisions based on whether or not I thought it would make a good story sometime in the future.

"Just wear something skin-tight and bring heels," she said. "Don't worry about your hair and makeup because no one's going to see it, anyway. Just wear your hair down."

Hot Girls always wear their hair down. When was the last time you saw someone with a ponytail on the cover of *Cosmo*?

When Kristen posted the production stills of my stripping scene on Facebook, I acted mildly embarrassed so people wouldn't think I was too brazen, but I was privately thrilled to see this side of myself get let out of hiding.

"Everyone is asking me, 'Who's that girl?'" Kristen's eyes were shining.

"Liam was desperate to know," she continued. "So I told him and he couldn't believe it. He's totally into you now."

I smirked. People always underestimate me because of the Jane Austen Effect, but there I was, finally coming out as a sex goddess.

"You were amazing in that scene," Liam said at the next party. He leaned in close to be heard over the music. "I had no idea that could be you."

I pointed my toes toward him and ran my fingers through my long hair. He was tall and handsome; I looked up at him through three coats of mascara and shrugged. It felt like I stood there like that for hours, but it was probably no more than five or ten minutes, and in *all* that time Liam never tried to kiss me.

I wasn't in the mood to waste my time so, disappointed, I went back to an old standby: Ryan. By then we'd started kissing semi-regularly at parties, almost out of habit, so it really wasn't a big deal anymore. Ryan had a reputation for making out with a different girl every weekend, but he had actually become one of my closest guy friends, making it feel comfortable and safe.

So comfortable and safe that I always ignored the fact that Ryan was a terrible kisser. He would rub his beard all over my face and lick the makeup off my chin, but it's better to have a bad kiss than no kiss. Because after all: "I consider alcohol wasted if I don't make out with anyone."

I said this during a PGA to make my friends laugh. PGA was short for "Post-Game Analysis." Every morning after a party, my roommate and I would roll out of bed into our sweatpants and meet up with the rest of our girlfriends to hash out the events of the previous evening. Who went home with whom. Who broke the towel rack in the bathroom. Who couldn't remember bits of the night and needed to be caught up.

I rolled my eyes when I said it, but what was the point of getting dressed up and pouring poison down your throat if you weren't going to get a little action?

The girls all laughed like I'd hoped. Maybe I had gotten to the bottom of why we all binge-drank on a regular basis. After all, when was the last time any of these single girls had sex sober?

Alcohol gave me confidence. It made me feel sexy. It made it easier to talk to people I didn't know very well. It made me *fun*.

I believe we drank for all those reasons, but it wasn't something we discussed or acknowledged openly. Until I opened my big mouth and said what I believed we were all thinking: drinking makes it easier to hook up with guys.

We were all still laughing at my wry-but-truthful humour when one of the girls whipped out a Sharpie and a piece of paper. She copied down what I said and taped it up on the wall of their kitchen with my name attached.

Sure, I thought. *Let everyone know I'm funny and can take an honestly self-aware look at the realities of campus culture.* I was sure I wasn't the only one who used alcohol to help their sex life.

Case in point: a few weeks later the boys who lived down the road announced their first big blow-out party.

"It's a *Jersey Shore* party!" my roommate Jess said.

"What's that?"

"You know, like, *Jersey Shore* themed."

I didn't know, but a little Googling taught me everything I needed.

The Jersey Shore, in addition to being a coastal location somewhere in the northeastern United States, was a popular reality TV show from 2009 to 2012 that seems to have been culturally significant enough to prompt a 2018 reboot. I've never seen the show, but my understanding is that it followed a group of twenty-something Italian Americans who lived in the same house, partied a lot, and slept around. I imagined it sort of like *Girls Gone Wild,* but with boys, too, and politically incorrect Italian stereotypes.

After just a few minutes online, I'd learned enough to know that nothing in my wardrobe would be remotely suitable for this theme and there was no way I could pull off that much fake tanner. I raided my closest until I found a long skin-tight red shirt. I usually wore it with jeans, but it was made out of some strange fabric that made it possible for me to pull it down just far enough to cover my behind. I didn't even bother with self-tanner, but I went heavy on the eye makeup and managed to create a pouffy pompadour on the top of my head without too much backcombing. I didn't know if I would have fit in on *Jersey Shore,* but I figured not wearing pants was a good place to start.

It was the middle of winter in North Toronto and the snow made it impossible to walk anywhere in the three-inch heels I planned on wearing. I pulled thick sweatpants and a winter parka on top of my "dress" and threw my heels into a bag. I was going to have to show up in winter boots and a full snowsuit.

Back then, we never went anywhere without pre-drinking at Headquarters. HQ was a townhouse five minutes from campus where most of the girls in my clique lived. My roommate and I schlepped our high heels and our plastic bottles of grapefruit juice and vodka across the frozen tundra until we found ourselves in the brightly lit kitchen at Headquarters. There on the wall, right by the door, a sign: I CONSIDER ALCOHOL WASTED IF I DON'T MAKE OUT WITH ANYONE.

I poured myself a shot.

I looked around and realized I probably hadn't dressed nearly trashy enough. I was not the only girl who had thought to wear a shirt as a dress, but the others were also busy painting on extra cleavage with makeup. My shirt had elbow-length sleeves and didn't cut low enough to really show off my breasts. I comforted myself with the fact that I was the skinniest girl in the room and the Pill had given me an almost cartoonish breast-to-waist-to-hip ratio. We all got together for a group photo and I made sure to stand like I was auditioning for a spot on a billboard: chest out, tummy in, back arched, duck face. Somewhere, in a dark corner of the internet, this picture still exists. Ten points for anyone who can find it.

Some of my current guilt at having been an insecure, looks-obsessed asshole was abated when I stumbled across a reference to a study conducted at two universities by Dorothy Holland and Margaret Eisenhart. These anthropologists found that "a woman's status on campus was determined almost exclusively by her perceived level of physical attractiveness among men."[5] Okay, so I wasn't the only looks-obsessed asshole on campus.

Back at HQ, we threw down a few more vodka shots and set off. We poured into the *Jersey Shore* party in a blur. We flung our sweatpants and winter boots everywhere, tugged on our shirts to make sure they were still covering our bums, threw ourselves into the arms of our hosts, and demanded that we all start drinking immediately to celebrate our arrival.

I don't know how many more drinks we had before I heard a new voice behind me.

"Hi, what's your name?"

I didn't know where he came from, but he was tall and I thought he seemed relatively good-looking. It was hard to tell in the dark, but I was intrigued.

"Nellwyn, what's yours?"

"Tim."

Tim. Tim. Must remember, new friend Tim.

When I close my eyes to picture him, it's like holding up a candle in an unlit room. The light flickers briefly across the angles of his face, but everything else is dark. I remember short, brown hair, big eyes, a wide smile, and the next thing I remember is kissing him in the middle of the kitchen. My unfortunate habit of engaging in drunken PDA combined with that quote hanging on the wall at HQ was quickly starting to topple my reputation as a good girl.

Time: 30 minutes. People kissed: 1.

In the middle of what I remember as a perfectly decent make-out, I felt a hand on my shoulder that couldn't possibly belong to Tim. I turned around and inches from my face was my classmate Kristen. Before I had time to respond, she planted a big kiss right on my lips. I'd never kissed a girl before, but it really wasn't that different, and besides, Tim was still standing right behind me. Watching us.

What the hell, I thought, and kissed her back.

I wondered if I was about to have some kind of sexual awakening. Maybe I wasn't meant to pursue boys after all? But all I could think while I kissed her was *Is he watching?*

I guess that's how I knew I was straight. And as a bonus I misguidedly thought I'd figured out a great way to get guys to pay attention to me.

"He's an asshole," Kristen whispered in my ear. "Don't go home with him."

This was a time when we girls were expected to listen to our friends without question. It wasn't only the Clique Knows What's Best. It was the Clique Knows What's Best *for You.* So I immediately took Kristen's hand and we giggled our way to the other side of the house, leaving Tim behind. I was disappointed — he seemed nice, but the night was still very young.

Time: 33 minutes. People kissed: 2.

I wandered through the party, drinking my vodka grapefruit juice and floating in and out of circles. My girlfriends were all either outside smoking or having their own public make-out sessions in different corners of the house. I made a brief appearance out on the porch where five people who "don't smoke" were all sharing a single cigarette. I took a few drags when it came around to me and washed the taste of ash down my throat with a little more of my homemade cocktail.

So much of how we construct and view our "wanted self" is defined by our social groups. Without trying or realizing it, I had fallen into a group that, like so many on college campuses, reinforced the connection between carefree sexuality and belonging. And the belonging wasn't really about belonging in the clique; I knew my friends didn't care if I wanted to be a virgin until marriage or not. It was a bigger, subconscious, and more abstract kind of belonging: belonging to adulthood, to empowerment, to freedom and liberation.

When it comes to hooking up and the pursuit of a sexually experienced and liberated identity, "the cultural norms that we live by can dictate how people act in a given situation." Nothing exists in a vacuum; society provides a social script for us to follow.[6]

The often-cited Online College Social Life Survey concluded that 72 percent of college students had engaged in a hookup by senior year.[7] Another study conducted by the Institute for American Values found that hooking up has "largely replaced traditional dating on college campuses," and that 91 percent of college women believed that hookups occurred "very often" or "fairly often" on their campus.[8]

The girls in my social circle were hooking up regularly and every detail was discussed at our Post-Game Analyses. While I like to think we came up with the term "PGA," we certainly weren't the only ones to use gossip and the lack of privacy in our social group to fuel the fires of hookup culture. Research done by sociologist Kathleen Bogle found that, for college students, "discussing what other students were doing sexually was a common pastime."[9] Bogle makes the connection between this lack of privacy and the pervasiveness of hookup culture: when hooking up becomes part of the publicly known social script, college students are more likely to participate in that script because "that's the thing to do."[10]

Casual sex was the norm, and since I wasn't having any sex at all, I felt like I was missing out. Many years later, it's comforting to know I wasn't the only one who felt that way. But at the time, I was deeply conflicted. I knew I was missing out on sex and dating, and I wanted desperately to experience those things. But at nineteen and in only my second year of university, I still wanted sex and dating to go together, at least at first. All my friends who were now having casual sex had lost their virginity to someone they were dating. It wasn't that I thought virginity was particularly special, or that I had to be in love or even in a relationship, but I thought that a one-night stand for my first time wouldn't be a good idea. I didn't know what I was doing, after all, so I thought that first going on one or two dates with the guy would make it easier to trust and communicate with him. I didn't think it was too much to ask, and I didn't think I had unrealistic romanticized notions.

Since I had a self-imposed restriction on one-night stands, I couldn't really fully participate in the social script, which made me feel even more like an outsider. I was behind the crowd again and still struggling to catch up by completing the right milestones in the right order. And yet, because I wasn't keeping pace properly, I had to balance the push-pull between what I wanted and what I thought I should be doing. At the same time, no one had ever asked me out on a date and not stood me up or abandoned me halfway through. Because that had crippled my self-esteem, the only thing I could think to do to feel better about myself and fit in was to enjoy some of the preamble that comes before casual sex. After all, people define "hooking up" as anything from just kissing to full-on intercourse. All the making out I was doing at parties was enough to mean that I was included and participating enthusiastically in the social script, while still holding out hope that one day — someday — I would go on a real date.

Back inside the *Jersey Shore* party, I stumbled into Nate. He was a couple years older than me and a member of the most prestigious boys clique in the theatre department, but had also always been incredibly nice. We kissed for a while in the line for the bathroom, but I wasn't really committed. I had my eye on someone else.

Time: 2 hours. People kissed: 3.

Cody was one of the first guys on my radar from the very beginning of university, and at the *Jersey Shore* party he was single for the first time since we'd met. He was very rugged, a bona fide cowboy from Alberta. I pressed him up against the living room wall and we were finally, finally kissing. I don't know if it was the anticipation, the binge-drinking, or a simple lack of chemistry, but it was not what I expected. In fact, it was seriously disappointing kissing. I couldn't get rid of the image that I was trying to wrangle a boa constrictor into submission with my mouth. I twirled my hair around my fingers and tried to stand seductively, but instead I crashed hard against the wall. It was getting difficult to stand up straight for longer than a few seconds. I did a quick scan around the party and realized all my friends had disappeared.

Fuck.

It's time to go home.

Despite being a university neighbourhood, we lived in a dangerous part of town and travelled strictly in packs after dark. The fact that all my friends had abandoned me at the party says a lot about how drunk we all really were. Still, I wasn't overly concerned as I leaned against the wall for support. I figured that since the night was winding down and I'd clearly finished it with Cody, he was obligated to walk me home. But then I heard his friend who'd been watching us kiss make some comment about how we were really going to town, and I felt the need to clarify.

"I'm not going to have sex with you tonight!" I shouted.

Despite how drunk I was, I could see the look in their eyes. It's the look men get when they think a woman has slipped into "crazy" territory.

My propensity for kissing random boys in public had established me as a little bit loose, and now that I'd told the whole room I would be going to bed alone, I'd also given myself a reputation as a little bit of a tease.

"What?" I said. "So. What? I'm not going to have sex with you *tonight*, but I need you to walk me home. What's the big deal?"

Cody and his friend looked at each other. Something was going on. Something more than "this drunk girl is acting crazy."

"Don't worry," Cody said. "I'm not interested in going home with you."

Well, fine then.

I stumbled toward the door and sifted through the pile of shoes, looking for my sweatpants and boots. Suddenly I spotted a classmate who I knew lived on campus, too.

"Are you leaving?" I asked.

"Yeah." He's a minimalist.

"I'm walking home with you. I mean, do you mind walking me home? We're going the same way."

"Yeah. Yeah, sure."

I spent most of the walk ranting about how you can't even get a guy you make out with to walk you home these days.

My bodyguard stayed pretty quiet, and dropped me off at the front door of my building.

"Are you sure you're okay?" he asked.

"What? Me! Yeah! Yeah of course, why wouldn't I be?"

"You just seem a little ... never mind, have a good night."

Time: 4 hours ... 5? People kissed: 4.

It turned out I left my high heels on the floor at the party and had to make a detour on my way to the next morning's PGA to pick them up. I showed up at HQ in the bright winter light oddly similarly to how I'd shown up a mere twelve hours before: in sweatpants, carrying my heels in bag, and stone-cold sober. I flopped into a chair at the kitchen table and poured myself a big mug of tea.

About half the girls in our clique had had sex that night and all but one had a decent kiss before heading home. A better than average ratio for a night's work. Two of the girls had actually traded hookups and each slept with a guy the other had had sex with the weekend before.

We were starting to realize we were losing track. Despite meticulous recapping at our PGAs, we were getting confused about who had slept with whom and who had made out with whom. Being the stellar high-achieving academics that we were, we resorted to the ultimate scientific method: colour-coded charts. Ellie wrote the names of everyone in our regular crowd in a circle and drew lines connecting us all based on our past liaisons. When she'd finished, she taped it up on the wall right next to my now-famous quote. I stepped back and looked. Despite still being a virgin, I had a shocking number of lines fanning out from my name. I was the runner-up in the game of promiscuity and I'd never even seen an adult man without his clothes on. For some reason, I felt pleased. If I were ever concerned about my popularity, the proof of my social status was hanging right there on the wall. I was sexually desirable and each one of those lines on that chart was proof that I was attractive enough for a man to want me. At least for a little while. That's the screwed-up kind of validation a girl like me needs when she's nineteen and still hasn't ever been on a real date.

Sex often serves as a barometer of personal success; it's a symbol that validates, not only our physical attractiveness but how desirable, accomplished, and well-adjusted we are as human beings. Although it's a very flawed way of looking at the world, desirability on all levels and "fitting in" are not easy ideas to let go of.

From a scientific standpoint, a study on the relationship between sex and social status done by psychologists at Yale University found that students "who reported sexual activity had high levels of reputation-based popularity."[11]

We left our sex chart up on the wall for all to see.

We are postmodern feminists and we are not ashamed of our sexual liberation. We are in control of our bodies and we have no regrets.

All that was true, but the chart also made us seem cool, popular, desirable, fun, and beautiful. What we didn't realize was that we would never be truly liberated until we learned to separate our sex lives from our sense of self.

The kitchen at the next party was dark and full of strangers; only one theatre student lived in this house and she'd never hosted anything before. Thankfully this party didn't have a theme beyond "happy birthday so-and-so," and it was relatively uneventful. I was definitely wearing pants when I spotted a cute, dark-haired man standing by himself across the room. He looked lonely and out of place, so I walked right up to him, drink in hand, and he wedged himself up against the fridge.

"Where are we?" he asked me. "I have no idea how to get home from here."

"There's a bus, I think. But it'll take you, like, two hours to get back downtown."

"I feel really old," he said.

"Why?" I asked. "How old are you?"

"Twenty-eight."

Shit. What is this guy doing at a college party?

"My friend brought me here," he added quickly. "I didn't realize we were going to a college party, but I think we're too old to be here."

You are, I thought. *But you know it and your attendance wasn't voluntary, so it's okay.* I was starting to get excited about the possibility of dating a real man.

We spent the whole night chatting, but he never moved from his spot up against the fridge and our lips never met. I was not drunk enough to make the first move with a real adult man who was a touring musician on top of everything.

In the middle of my flirtation, I saw Sarah and Ellie coming down the stairs from the bedrooms with two of their past hookups, Andrew and Ian.

Oh god, here we go again.

Sarah came up behind me and whispered in my ear, "We're leaving. NOW."

Once again, I blindly followed the Girl Code.

"I have to go," I told the man reluctantly. I barely had time to get the words out; Sarah had already grabbed my hand and was pulling me out the door.

"What's going on?" I asked. "I really liked that guy!"

"We're leaving, and you're coming with us."

Sarah was using a tone that told me not to ask questions.

Time: 3–4 hours. People kissed: 0.

I followed them through the rows of identical townhouses until we fell into drunken pile on the sofa at Andrew's: Sarah, Ellie, Ian, Andrew, and me.

The other four started kissing and I was tangled somewhere in between them all.

"I just realized," someone said. "We've all kissed each other before."

"No, we haven't," I said. "Andrew and I have never kissed."

He looked at me and shrugged. His shrug said, *We can fix that right now if you want.*

I shrugged, too, and leaned in.

That was that taken care of.

It wasn't much later before someone realized we can't say we've all made out with each other unless we include girl-on-girl. So we took care of that, too.

All in one move, we'd proven we were sexually adventurous, liberated, and willing to fulfill stereotypical male fantasies by playing right into the Male Gaze without thinking twice. *Score.* That's one more point for Team Fucked Up Validation.

"We are not all having sex tonight," I said. I was determined not to lose my virginity in a five-person orgy with my friends.

"God, no, of course not."

But we didn't stop kissing each other.

"We're not having sex tonight."

But we kept rotating partners.

"We're not having sex tonight."

But we ended up in the bedroom.

Sarah, Ellie, and Ian were together on one side of the room, and I was with Andrew on the other. I could feel his hands getting bolder.

I am not losing my virginity in an orgy.

But I didn't want to stop. We were drunk, but I didn't think we were *that* drunk.

It all seemed very wild at the time, but before anything went beyond what you'd see on prime-time television, Ian's head started bobbing down toward his chest.

"Are you all right?" Sarah asked.

"Yeah, yeah, I'm fine."

But his eyes were closed and he couldn't hold up his head.

The spell was broken; it was time to go home.

Time: 1 hour. People kissed: 4.

Sarah texted me the next morning before we even had a chance to get together for our PGA.

"Thank god you were there last night. You were our saving grace."

If I hadn't been there, the other four would have quickly coupled off and had sex, even though that wasn't what either of the girls claimed to want in the light of day.

"Yeah, well, I'm glad I could help out."

That afternoon after our PGA, as we lay on the living room floor at HQ doing our homework, someone got bored.

"Let's go on Chatroulette!" one of the girls suggested.

Chatroulette is a website that had a brief vogue while I was in undergrad. It's a simple video chatroom that matches you with random people all over the world. The only things you can do are talk to the person you are matched with or skip ahead to be matched with someone new. At the time, it was used mostly by men who wanted to masturbate publicly without the risk of getting arrested. And stupid college students, apparently.

"Why, what's the point?" I asked.

"It's hilarious! You can see so many dicks!"

One of the girls ran upstairs and got her laptop. She logged on and everyone crowded around the camera. We cycled through a bunch of boring-looking people sitting by themselves in dimly lit rooms. We had a bit of fun chatting with a group of freshmen college boys somewhere in the States who had no idea what cunnilingus was. Educating them was kind of a public service.

"This is boring," someone said. "I want to see some dicks. Put Nellwyn in the front. She's got the biggest boobs."

On my own, I would never have used the internet to let a stranger masturbate to my face. But my friends made it seem like it would be fun, so refusing to participate would inherently make me "not fun." It wasn't until I began looking back on these moments that I realized there is *nothing* normal about letting your friends talk you into becoming the image some stranger jerks off to. That is definitely not the kind of validation I want.

I don't remember how much later it was that Kristen came over and dropped the biggest bomb to land on our class all year. Kristen, famous for having turned me into a stripper, was also famous for her mysterious ability to make all men want to sleep with her. Or so she claimed whenever there happened to be a lull in conversation.

"Andrew has rated every girl in our class from one to ten. You know, like, in level of attractiveness," she said, sitting on the floor of my roommate's bedroom. "And he told me what everyone's number is."

It was like offering raw antelope to a pride of starving lions.

"Seven is his cut-off for whether or not he'll sleep with you," she continued. "He doesn't sleep with girls who are lower than a seven."

We shouldn't ask. We shouldn't want to know. But Kristen jumped right in without needing any encouragement.

"You and I are both eights," Kristen said, pointing to my roommate. "Nellwyn is an eight point five. And you should feel good about that," she said to me. "Because the only girls he ranked higher than you are Ellie and Dina. He said they are both nines, but, I mean, he's slept with Ellie and Dina is a model, so that's fair."

Unlike many of the girls in our class, I wasn't devastated by my number, but I was crushed by what Andrew had done to us.

Is this what we were reduced to? Andrew was our friend, our classmate, our comrade-in-arms in the trenches of theatre school. We were a group of intelligent, driven women who'd beaten hundreds of people to be one of only twenty students selected for our class. We weren't just classmates who shared a semester before moving back into the anonymous sea of university students. We were a tight-knit group in a specialized program who were going to spend our entire undergrad together; we were supposed to support each other, to allow each other to be emotionally vulnerable in the name of one day becoming great artists. But with a whisper of a number, Andrew broke that bond and many of us were reduced to tears.

We drank and partied and made sex charts so everyone knew how desirable we were because deep down we all wanted to feel pretty and popular. I had ugly thoughts about how I was skinnier and had bigger breasts than my friends because I really thought they were more beautiful than me, more sexually savvy, and more desired by men.

As disgusted as I was with Andrew's objectification of his friends, I still felt good about scoring high; I couldn't help it. I made out with boys because it made me feel good about myself to be desired. I drank because I didn't have the confidence to approach men without alcohol.

"I think you should start kissing people when you're sober so you don't feel so much pressure to kiss people when you're drunk," Dina said to me after the number scandal. Dina was very smart and very perceptive. But she was a model, so what did she know about struggling to get attention from men?

All I could think was *But no one wants to kiss me when I'm sober.*

CHAPTER 8

I DIDN'T PAY MUCH ATTENTION to Nate when I first met him. He was a few years older than everyone else in our program, twenty-three or twenty-four to our eighteen and nineteen. He was very popular and threw great parties. He was a little rough around the edges, with calluses on his fingers, but he dressed well and he was kind. If he went to Tim Hortons during a lecture break, he would offer to pick something up for the professor. Not to gain any extra points, but just because he understood that a prof swarmed with questions from anxious students during his only ten minutes off might be desperate for a little caffeine.

I liked Nate, but I didn't really have any big feelings for him. He reminded me of my older brother: strong, safe, happy-go-lucky, and gentle, but so de-sexualized to me that he might as well have been made of stone. Which isn't at all to say that he was unattractive, I just never thought of him that way.

That's probably part of why I didn't feel committed when we made out at the *Jersey Shore* party. I don't remember how it started, but since we were both in line for the bathroom it felt like little more than a fun way to pass the time. I didn't think much about him again until my roommate Jess brought him up one evening after coming home from the campus pub. She'd gone for a happy hour beer after class, but I'd gone straight home for some reason and was busy making dinner in our tiny kitchen when she came in.

"Your name came up a lot at the bar today," she said, taking off her coat.

"Why?" I asked with trepidation, fearing the worst.

"Nate couldn't stop taking about you, how great you are …"

"Really?" I asked, completely surprised.

"I think he really likes you," Jess concluded with a look that said I should expect more from him in the near future.

I hardly knew what to think, let alone what to say. I couldn't quite wrap my head around the idea that a guy might really like me before 10:00 p.m. and without hard liquor. Could this be it? What I'd been waiting and hoping for? I forgot all about my lack of attraction to Nate and focused instead on the glimmering kernel of hope, praying that Jess hadn't misunderstood and trying to keep my expectations low. It was no more than a few days later when Nate's name popped up on my Facebook notifications. It was a private message: "Hey, I was wondering if maybe you'd like to get a coffee sometime?"

There it was. It looked like it might really happen. My first proper date that might not end in disaster.

We agreed to meet at a campus coffee shop in the theatre building after class, and though this was largely uncharted territory for me, I left like I had a decent handle on what I was doing. I showed up ten minutes early and bought myself a tea so that there wouldn't be any haggling over who would pay $2.50 to caffeinate the other. The question of money was what stressed me out the most about dating. A blip of an encounter at a bar downtown not long before had left me confused and gun-shy.

My friends and I had taken a Friday night and committed to the one-hour journey downtown so we could try some new bars and hopefully meet some new boys. The journey to a popular hot spot in the Annex turned out to be worth it when a group of cute young professionals not long out of undergrad themselves joined our table. One guy and I hit it off right away. He was an investment banker also originally from a small town who shared my love of horseback riding. As my vodka cranberry slid low and the ice-cubes clicked louder against the sides of the glass, Mr. Equestrian offered to buy my next drink. I refused; he offered again in case I was just being polite, and I refused again very emphatically. By this time, we'd made our way up to the bar together. I paid for my second vodka cran and he bought himself another pint. I smiled at him, thinking we would go back to our table and resume our conversation about show jumping. Instead, he gave me a small nod and a tiny smile before disappearing into some other part of the crowded bar. Yet again, I wondered what had happened, what I'd done wrong. My friends were quick to enlighten me.

"He thought you didn't like him," they said.

To me, letting a man buy me a drink implied that I wasn't independent, and the whole ritual felt left over from a sexist era I refused to perpetuate. To him, asking to buy me a drink was asking to spend a little more time together, to continue to get to know each other, to see if we liked each other. I'm not at all saying that I would have felt I owed him anything whatsoever if I'd accepted, but I didn't know that him asking was supposed to be code for "I might like you, do you think you might like me, too?" Completely unaware, my refusal had amounted to him getting the message that I wanted him to leave me alone. And, being a gentleman, he did. So, what was I supposed to do? How was I going to be an independent, financially empowered feminist while still letting men know that I was interested in them? Did I have to let them buy me a drink? How do we translate our ideologies into real, personal moments? Moments that are inherently full of all the messiness that comes with being human and vulnerable and hoping that you might really have met someone special. Unable to reconcile the extremely complex gender, social, political, economic, and personal dynamics, I opted to avoid the issue of who would pay wherever possible.

So, I showed up ten minutes early to my date with Nate to be nearly guaranteed to arrive first. I settled in at a table with my cup of Earl Grey and opened the book I'd brought along so it didn't look at all like I was waiting for someone. Nate walked in and from that moment on, dating was what it's supposed to be — or what I thought it was supposed to be at least. We talked about our families and our hobbies; we went to the movies, danced together at parties, and sat next to each other at the bar on pub night. He was textbook and so was our budding relationship. I should have known it couldn't possibly be that easy, maybe for other girls, but not for me.

I wanted to want him so desperately. I told myself I was just new to this world and inexperienced, too anxious for my own good and trapped in my head. But when he came up behind me and kissed me on the cheek, I wanted to pull away. I fought myself and I felt torn in pieces. He walked me home in the rain and reached out for my hand, stopping me and pulling me toward him.

"Let's kiss in the rain," he said.

I knew it was supposed to be romantic. I was supposed to feel special in this picture-perfect movie moment, but all I felt was cold and wet. *What is wrong with me?* I asked myself over and over again. *Why couldn't I like him? Why couldn't I sink into this relationship?* There was absolutely nothing wrong, except that I didn't feel anything for him.

And since he was perfect, there obviously had to be something wrong with me if I couldn't fall for the great guy who treated me well and clearly liked me a lot.

The wind picked up and I pulled away from his arms, blaming the cold and the rain and moving once again toward home with my hands now in my pockets. At the edge of campus, we reached my building and Nate came upstairs with me. Still in our wet clothes, we fell onto the bed and kissed. It was late and I was so tired. After all those years of dreaming, I wanted nothing more that night than to be alone.

"You should go," I said gently.

He nodded to show he'd heard me, but his eyes moved toward the window where the rain had become a thunderstorm.

"Can I stay?" he asked quietly.

I hesitated.

"Not tonight."

"We don't have to do anything," he added quickly. "We can just go to sleep. It's so awful outside."

I used my tiny twin-size bed as an excuse.

"This bed is way too small for us," I said. "We're both too tall."

"We can fit," he said softly. "What if I hold you really close?"

He put his arms around me and we both turned to the side so he could show me how much space there was and how cozy we would be together under the blankets with the storm pounding against the windows. I knew I wouldn't be able to sleep. I couldn't explain why I felt the way I did, but I didn't want this perfectly lovely boy to spend the night. I was in utter agony, but I was firm.

"I don't think so; I think you should go home."

Reluctantly, but not unkindly, Nate put on his shoes and kissed me goodbye, promising to call me in the morning. I stood at my window and watched the rain beat against the glass in the darkness, imagining I could see his silhouette walking away on the street below, his shoulders hunched against the cold and the wind.

. . ● . .

Nate and I kept dating, and I kept hoping to feel something, anything, different than what I felt. He invited me over to his place where he had made beautifully roasted chicken thighs for us to share for dinner, but I'd already eaten before leaving the house. I couldn't eat in front of guys back then, my throat closed up and my stomach turned at the thought of food, or rather at the thought of a man watching, cataloguing, and categorizing the food I put in my mouth. Nate looked disappointed when I told him I'd already eaten, and he refused to eat without me even though I encouraged him, knowing he must have been hungry.

We were in his bedroom this time when I felt myself pulling away again. Every time things started to go a little further, I moved away. I knew I was hurting him and confusing him, but my body felt out of my control. No matter how much I wanted to want him, I couldn't bring myself to have sex with him when I didn't feel anything. Not only did I feel neutral toward him romantically, my body kept actively pulling me away, like it had some kind of aversion to this beautiful boy whom I cared about and whom I thought cared about me. Finally, I stood up and left, looking away from the confusion and hurt in his eyes. Confusion and hurt that didn't want to push me, that was respectful of my feelings and my boundaries, but that showed me he really didn't understand.

Neither did I.

. . ● . .

Despite the fact that I had listened to my body and stayed true to myself, I felt guilty and broken. I called my mom, who always had good advice and who knew a lot about men. I told her I was pretty sure I had to break up with him, knowing I could only torment us both for so long. I was also starting to think that after two months of dating, I wasn't going to begin to feel any differently about him.

For perhaps the first time in my life, my mother completely failed to understand me.

"Why do you want to break up with him?" she asked me. "What's wrong?"

"Nothing," I replied honestly. "I just don't feel anything for him; it doesn't feel right."

"But why?"

"I don't know," I repeated. "I wish I did."

"Look, Nell," she said to me. "Not every guy is going to be the one. Don't overthink this. My first boyfriend in high school wasn't very good-looking at all; I was way out of his league. But he was nice and he treated me well, so we had sex and it was great. He was a great *first* boyfriend."

I started crying on the other end of the phone.

"But I don't want to do that," I said.

"You can break up with him if you want to, I'm just saying … it sounds like you're telling me he's a good guy."

He was.

But I couldn't do it.

• • • • •

The foundation of feminism is meant to empower and liberate women so that we only have sex when we truly want to. My mom is an ardent feminist, there is no question about it, so I genuinely didn't understand our phone call. The message I was getting, not just from her but from the surrounding culture, was that I should sleep with Nate, and that I should *want* to sleep with Nate.

He checked all the right boxes, so what was the problem? Didn't I want to express my sexuality? Wasn't I supposed to be free — thanks to my mother's generation — from sexual repression? Was I harbouring some internalized self-hatred and shame put into my head by the patriarchy?

Feminism has countless definitions and means something different to different people. At the same time, a partial definition I think we can all agree on is that feminism is the liberation of women from the values and systems of the patriarchy.[1] For centuries, the patriarchy told us not to have sex unless under very specific conditions, to be ashamed and uneducated about our bodies, to repress and hide from our sexuality. To liberate myself from these values and structures, I had gotten the message that I should do the opposite and adhere to a new social system. The rules had changed, but they hadn't been eliminated altogether. What did it mean for me to break up with Nate and keep waiting to have sex? The message I felt I'd received was that it meant I was scared and overthinking everything, over-evaluating risk, internalizing patriarchal values, or shutting the door on important life experiences based on shame, repression, and anxiety. I was faulty because I still hadn't learned how to *relax and have fun.*

I know we all need to let loose and be spontaneous and follow our instincts from time to time. But when did *thinking* become such a dirty word? I've heard it my whole life. "You think too much." "You're overthinking this." "Stop thinking about it." But thinking is a right and a privilege women haven't always had, not publicly or in a way that could be acted upon.

At the same time, parts of me *weren't* overthinking. I knew what was right for me, and my body was telling me in no uncertain terms. When, without thinking about it at all, I pulled my hips away from Nate and retreated to the other side of the bed, some part of my inner core was telling me that this was not what I wanted. It wasn't at all because I wasn't ready to have sex, and that's part of what confused me so much. I *was* ready, but I wanted to feel my heart skip a beat. I wanted to feel like I was melting, like I did when Tyler kissed me up against the kitchen sink.

The ideology and social mores that told me I should want a guy like Nate, the ones that made me feel defective for *not* feeling a flutter in my chest when he entered a room, made me question what I knew in my body. But when you're deciding something so personal and intimate as who to share your body with, why shouldn't you think about it carefully and take the time to fully analyze your feelings?

Almost ten years later, I have no regrets because I thought through everything that was going on inside me. I questioned myself, but ultimately I made the choice to listen to my body and to my gut instincts. Looking back at all the confusion, uncertainty, and guilt I felt at the time, and the pervasive and continued feeling that there was something defective about me, I wonder where I went wrong. How could I have saved myself all that torment?

In a postmodern feminist world where I am supposed to feel free and empowered to trust my instincts and make my own personal and individual choices no matter what they may be, how did I so grossly misinterpret my own liberation? Why did it take me so long to do what I *knew* was right for me?

There is often a clash that happens when an ideology or an internalized social convention butts up hard against real practical experience. When thinking about and looking at my relationship with Nate, I felt that there was a right choice, a clear path I should take, but that was not the path my heart or my body wanted to follow. My conversation with my mother only confirmed this idea. But my mother didn't know what my body was telling me and she only saw her overly cautious daughter running away from the possibility of love. All mothers want their daughters to be happy and safe, and great-on-paper guys like Nate offer that whole package. But only if the great-on-paper guy is also the *right* guy, and that's not always something you can explain. Especially not over the phone to your mom at nineteen years old.

For so many women in so many circumstances, sexual freedom and liberation means that you're being active, not passive; you're making the choice to be sexually active; you're getting ahead of the curve and taking control of the situation to fulfill your desires. But for me, with Nate, freedom meant walking away.

CHAPTER 9

T'S MANY YEARS LATER and I'm walking through my downtown Toronto neighbourhood on a rainy Wednesday afternoon. I'm doing a few errands before heading home to make a cup of tea when I start thinking about Kevin for the first time since undergrad. As I schlep through the remains of a late October hurricane with my rubber boots glistening and my scarf tied tightly over my hair, I realize that Kevin was exactly the kind of man I still consider "my type." If we all carry with us an internalized "wanted self," perhaps we also carry an internalized "wanted spouse." It didn't occur to me back in university, but Kevin and almost all the men I've since dated, or seriously considered dating, fit into this type.

Kevin was tall and effortlessly fit, without looking like a mannequin or a model. He looked like a real person, a handsome real person. He had the oval face and the strong jaw I found so appealing, and he looked older than most of the boys I knew. He was a little bit rugged and would sometimes go a few days without shaving, but his hair was always well-combed. He wore plaid and denim shirts right when they were coming back into fashion as hipster-chic. He was an alpha male without being a jock or a frat boy, and he was an artist at heart.

Picture Ryan Gosling.

So it goes without saying that Kevin was my ideal man when choosing from the pool of theatre students I knew. There were others who fit my type, but Kevin was by far the handsomest, and, in my mind, he definitely came the closest to Ryan Gosling. But, like with the real-life Ryan G., the timing never seemed to work out. He had a serious girlfriend from the moment I met him, which unfortunately made him all the more attractive. Proof that a guy can commit to a relationship gives him some serious bonus points, whether or not I'm actually looking to "settle down."

Now, before you get any ideas, I have *never* made a move on anyone who I knew was in a monogamous relationship. *Never.* So Kevin was in the "look but don't touch" category for the first half of my undergrad.

Until we came back to school for our third year and I heard that he and his girlfriend had broken up. The idea of being with him, which had always been relegated to a dark and dusty back corner of my imagination, was starting to creep slowly into the foreground of my fantasies.

By now, I was twenty.

And a virgin.

This might not be a big deal to a lot of people, but it was starting to become unbearable for me. I was ready to have sex. I'd been ready for a long time, and all I'd asked for was a guy who made my stomach flutter and who would take me out on a date first. I was convinced this wasn't unreasonable, but all my efforts had done nothing to yield the results I wanted.

Whatever ideals I'd had when I pictured losing my virginity seemed to be tied to some leftover patriarchal notion that it shouldn't be thrown away. I'd had enough of a feminist reality check to know that sex didn't need to occur within the confines of a long-term relationship and that there would be no candles or rose petals, but I had still internalized the patriarchal idea that a one-night stand was a bad choice for a first-timer. I thought if a guy bothered to take me out on a date first, it would mean he respected me a little, maybe even thought I was an interesting person, and that there was a slightly higher chance he would still like me in the morning.

But then again, was it the patriarchy telling me to wait for a date with a sense of chemistry or was it genuinely what I wanted for myself? Even after breaking up with Nate, I still felt conflicted and pulled between these different ideologies and where my self and my body fit in between them.

Before I could come to a conclusion, I turned twenty and everything changed.

Although I wouldn't become aware of it until several years later, *Globe and Mail* staff reporter Zosia Bielski wrote an article around this time titled "Protracted Virginity: For Those Who Wait, There's a Risk of Stigma." I find it interesting that this article was filed on the *Globe* website in the Health section under "Conditions." Apparently "protracted virginity" is considered a "health condition or concern." But what constitutes protracted virginity? Isn't something so personal clearly unquantifiable in that way? Doesn't it vary from person to person? Maybe in theory, but according to sexologist Jessica O'Reilly, "We're prescribed this cultural norm of sexuality. God forbid you have sex at sixteen, that's too young. But if you haven't had sex at twenty, well, that's too old."[1] In my experience, that timeline felt exactly correct. It was unspoken, but deeply understood among girls of my generation and social group that the "ideal" and most socially acceptable time to lose your virginity is between the ages of seventeen and nineteen. Perpetuating that cultural norm within the very same newspaper article, an adult (or "protracted") virgin is defined as anyone over the age of twenty. According to psychologist and professor Terry Humphreys, common reasons for protracted virginity include religious beliefs, a higher body mass index, and maturing later than your peer group.[2]

So the unfair and inaccurate yet general perception is that twenty-year-old virgins are religiously abstinent, fat, or socially inept. No wonder I was starting to feel more and more ashamed among my peers.

Sociologist Laura Carpenter is often credited as the researcher who defined the ways we understand virginity loss today. Her research shows that people look at virginity in one of three ways: as a gift, a stigma, or a rite of passage.*

People in the gift category see virginity as something special that can only be given once to a very important or loved person. Like with most gift-giving, reciprocity of some kind is expected and virginity is often exchanged for the gift of love or commitment.

Those in the stigma category feel embarrassed or ashamed of their virgin status and often express a desire to "get it over with." People in this category are more likely to lose their virginity to a friend or in a one-night stand.

But more than half the people Carpenter interviewed considered virginity loss to be a rite of passage, or a "step in the process of growing up."

"Despite perceiving virginity as essentially neutral in value, virtually every participant who framed virginity as a step in a process described the transition to non-virginity as inevitable and desirable in physical, emotional, or intellectual terms."[3]

Like any other step on the road to adulthood, becoming sexually active is seen by those in this category as a natural part of growing up and a way of gaining a very specific kind of adult knowledge.

---

* Carpenter also found an additional sub-category that applied only to members of particular religious groups who see virginity as an act of worship.

I had always been in the process-oriented category, but, as I got older, I felt that my age was involuntarily grafting social stigma on top of my own beliefs. Just like how I felt about my first kiss, most rites of passage have an expiration date before the stigmas start to sneak in like mould.

I started thinking maybe none of my previous ideas mattered all that much. That going on *one* date didn't really mean much of anything. If I was willing to sleep with a relative stranger after just a few hours of conversation over dinner, why couldn't I sleep with someone after a conversation over a few beers at one of our famous parties?

At some point not long after my twentieth birthday, I decided two things:

1. I didn't want to be a twenty-*one*-year-old virgin.
2. I would be happy to lose my virginity in a one-night-stand without any pretence of dating or romance, as long as I could be relatively sure the guy wasn't an axe murderer.

Considering almost everyone I knew was having sex with each other and we'd all been running in the same crowd for a couple of years, I thought having sex with someone in our circle would be relatively easy now that I'd made up my mind to do it. Bonus: I was 99 percent sure no one we knew had ever done hard time.

There's a perception that men are always "up for it," so it's easy for a girl to lose her virginity if she wants to, she just has to say the word. Interestingly enough, Laura Carpenter also came to this exact conclusion: "Men's relatively greater willingness to have sex outside of dating relationships appeared to enhance these women's ability to lose their virginity fairly rapidly once they elected to do so."[4]

Thus, another common belief is that female virgins are usually abstinent by choice, and up until my twentieth birthday I had been, to a certain degree. I didn't actually *want* to be abstinent, but I had turned down a few possibilities I wasn't interested in pursuing under the given circumstances. Now that I'd decided I was open to just about any circumstance, I was sure I'd be having sex in no time.

For our third year, my roommate and I moved off campus and into Headquarters with the rest of our clique. I suspected that not having to sign in guests at my dorm's front desk would be a nice transition into the next phase of adulthood, and not having to walk across that giant frozen campus parking lot would make getting to and from parties a whole lot easier.

Moving into Headquarters included a kind of orientation from our friends who'd already been in the house for a year.

These are your shelves in the fridge, this is where we keep the vacuum cleaner, and this is the list of guys you aren't allowed to sleep with.

The guys on the list were all part of the same friend group and they were kind of like the male equivalent of our clique. But one of my new roommates had recently been through a bad breakup with one of those guys so now the entire crowd was off-limits to the rest of us. I honestly thought they were joking. Particularly since the rest of the house rules were silly things like "Always make enough popcorn and tea for everyone," and "Share your nail polish." They weren't.

The first big party of the year was always a toga party. Like almost every other party we went to, it was held in one of the townhouses in our neighbourhood and everyone from the theatre department was invited by default.

Now that I lived at HQ, the party didn't just start with the pre-drink, it started with a getting-ready party. Whoever had the loudest speakers pumped music through the whole house while we took turns shaving our legs and doing our makeup. It would take us at least an hour to get ready for a party. Like any good debutante, I coated myself in something that smelled of coconut or vanilla and slipped into my sexiest underwear.

"I really don't want to have sex with anyone tonight," one of the girls said as we swapped places in front of the bathroom mirror. "So I didn't shave my vagina."

According to her, this was the only surefire way to make sure she went home alone. I, on the other hand, was ready to enact my new approach to hooking up and was prepared for anything.

"Ugh. I have to bring so many tampons to this party," said Sarah, shoving Tampax into her tiny purse.

"Um — why?"

"Because I'm going to be drunk and I'll have to pee a lot," she said.

"So?" I said.

"So I'll have to take out my tampon every time I have to pee."

"Umm … Sarah, do you know how your uterus works?"

It turns out she did not.

I suppose that by then we were used to having been failed by doctors, sex education teachers, and for girls like Sarah, even her mother. Dwelling on the gravity of Sarah's words would have been too sad, so all we did was turn the music up and double check that our house had plenty of emergency condoms on top of the fridge.

Normally we would get busy crawling through each other's closets to trade skirts and tank tops, but the dress code for this party was strict: togas only. We rounded up every white bedsheet we could find in the house and started experimenting. Turns out it's really hard to look cute in a sheet. It's also really hard to make sure that sheet covers everything you want covered and stays put after eight or nine drinks. It took some trial and error, but with our six or seven heads in the game we found a way to make it work. The key, in case anyone out there is wondering, is to tie the bedsheet over one shoulder, and use a belt to keep the sides closed and in place all night. A few strategic safety pins don't hurt, either. Before pinning myself into my toga, I dug through my closet to find my mother's vintage white slip, which she had finally given me outright; it was the one she never wore and that I used to borrow to dress up like a bride when I was five years old. I thought the slip was a good idea in case a corner of my new bedsheet-outfit fell out of place.

I styled some long brown tendrils around my face, pinned up half my hair so it looked vaguely goddess-like, and with some simple gold earrings I was feeling pretty good. Last year, I thought not wearing pants was risqué, but there I was wearing a bedsheet as a dress. It seemed like the perfect night to get laid.

This was our first excursion into party-land since I'd moved into Headquarters. As we were leaving, one of the girls realized that we didn't *all* need to bring our house keys, since we would be coming home together to the same place.

"Yeah! Great idea!"

Togas don't have pockets after all.

In retrospect, our past partying experience should have told me that the chances of us all going home together at the same time were very, *very* slim. But I think we'd already been through at least an hour of pre-drinking at this point, so we agreed: half of us would bring keys and the other half wouldn't. I don't like relinquishing control, so I brought my little key.

We arrived to find the usual crowd standing clustered around the front steps in the warmth of an early September night, catching up on summer gossip. Who'd broken up with whom. Who'd hooked up with a co-worker from camp who turned out to be a "stage 5 clinger." Who was already sleeping with a first-year.

I don't remember much about the early part of the night. This party only comes back to me in flashes. Perhaps that's typical of memory. Or perhaps that's typical of memories you make while swimming in alcohol.

There's a flash when I'm standing in the kitchen pouring myself a drink and chatting up the crowd.

There's a flash when I see Kevin standing in the backyard in front of the garage, looking handsome as ever. He was shirtless in jeans, with a blue towel draped around his torso. It was enough like a toga to make it past the front door and there was something I found incredibly sexy about a shirtless man in denim.

There's a flash when I'm flirting with Kevin in front of the garage with a drink in my hand.

There's a flash when he and I are making out in the alley between my friend's garage and the neighbour's.

There's a flash when Sarah's camera goes off and captures us kissing on digital film.

And there are a number of subsequent flashes when Sarah's camera goes off again and again and again.

"Stop documenting this!"

But I'm laughing and we don't stop kissing.

At some point Ellie stumbles past me.

"Give me your key. I'm going home."

There was no way I was leaving the party without being sure that Kevin was leaving with me.

"Okay," I said, handing it over. "But make sure you leave it under the mat so I can get in later."

"Yeah. Yeah, of course. I'll definitely leave it under the mat."

There's another big gap at this point in my memory, but I do remember walking home at the end of the night with Kevin. I started to sober up on the walk, so the rest of the night I remember very clearly.

"Didn't you give your key away?" he asked me. "How are you going to get in your house?"

"It's fine. I told Ellie to leave it under the mat."

"Well, I want to make sure you get inside okay," he said. "I'm not going to leave you locked out in your yard in the middle of the night."

"Don't worry," I said as I marched confidently to the mat in front of my back door. I pulled up the slightly damp and coarse wicker edge to stare at nothing but a big grey square of concrete.

"Oh my god, it's not here!" I shouted indignantly, holding the dirty mat up far away from my body.

"I can't believe her!" I said, stopping myself from going further and betraying my friend in front of a boy.

I knocked on the door and looked in through the window. I could see my key sitting on the kitchen table. Good for absolutely nothing.

There was a small light on in the kitchen, but the rest of the house was dark.

The adrenalin rush of standing stranded on my stoop at 3:00 a.m. jolted any residual alcohol out of my system. I banged on the door and shouted up at the closed windows, but it seemed like the alcohol had had the opposite effect on my roommates and they were all fast asleep. Suddenly, I realized Kevin was no longer standing behind me.

"Kevin?" I stepped back into the yard to look for him, but I was alone. "Where — *oh my god*, you're going to kill yourself!"

For some reason, I had thought to look up, and in the low light of a very early Sunday morning, I saw his silhouette climbing up the wall of my house. In shadow against the moon, his arms and legs reached out to span the three feet between my house and the neighbour's. Bent and tense, his legs stepped slowly up the brick inch by inch and his hands clung into the grout lines of the brick walls like they were rungs on a ladder.

"Come down," I shouted. "You're going to fall! You're going to hurt yourself!"

But he was making it look so easy, and before I could shout anything more, he was up and over, out of my sight and landing on the third-floor balcony right off Ellie's bedroom.

I was alone on my back stoop and suddenly everything was quiet. The buzz was gone; there was just a summer night. Dark. Quiet. And me.

I pictured him standing on the balcony, breathing heavily, adrenalin pumping as he knocked on the door. I imagined my roommates jumping out of bed with their hearts racing and I felt a twinge of guilt. But I looked through the window again and saw my key sitting on the table and I felt a little better. I just hoped they were all wearing pyjamas.

It wasn't long before I saw Kevin come downstairs and through the kitchen to let me in. He opened the door with a smile and I was hooked.

It seemed like there was nothing more romantic, or sexy, than a man who would scale a three-storey wall for me. I couldn't have asked for better foreplay.

I was feeling confident and calm, but not quite presumptuous enough to lead him directly upstairs to my bedroom. We made our way quickly to the living room. The curtains were drawn and the room was dark; his face was just a shadow close to mine. I sat down on the futon couch and pulled him toward me. He bent down and kissed me. With his knees between mine, he knelt forward and I leaned back on a pile of pillows.

A pile of pillows that started to move.

"Wha — Nellwyn?"

Turns out we had been making out on top of someone who'd fallen asleep on our futon couch.

"Ohmygod, I'm SO sorry.... Go back to sleep, we'll go upstairs!"

In my defence, it was very, *very* dark.

Up in my room with the door safely locked, we took off our togas and tumbled onto the pile of Swedish matchsticks I called a bed.

It wasn't long before I was wearing nothing but my vintage white slip, and Kevin was wearing nothing at all. His body was long and lean stretched out on my bed. My eyes grazed across his chest and stomach, down past his hips.

Okay.

It looks … nice.

Pretty much what I expected.

Tentatively, I knelt on top of him. He reached up and put his hands under my slip. I felt ready, but I knew I had to speak.

"Just so you know," I said, "I'm a virgin."

His hands came off me as he mumbled something I barely heard before rolling over to the other side of the bed and falling asleep. It all happened so fast I didn't even have time to think about adding a qualifying, "… but don't stop!"

I lay back and looked at the ceiling. A small beam of grey light was staring to glimmer against the plain white paint. It was creeping toward four in the morning and I knew he had to be up at eight for an all-day rehearsal on campus. I guessed he was tired or had a hangover threatening so I didn't think too much about falling asleep next to him, still wearing my slip and with all my makeup on.

Not tonight. But nothing is wasted.

A fact I didn't discover until later: many sexually active men don't want to have sex with a virgin.

Because losing your virginity is seen as a transformative experience, many men don't want the responsibility and pressure of changing an "innocent" virgin into a sexual being. That responsibility and pressure increases the older a virgin gets because of the stigmas we've seen earlier in this chapter. It's assumed that an "older" virgin is either waiting for something (or someone) *very* special and is looking for commitment, or that she is fundamentally flawed in some way since other men haven't already deemed her a worthy sexual conquest.

It's hard to find a lot of serious science on this social phenomenon, but anecdotal evidence is *everywhere*.

In a *Jezebel* article titled "How Guys Feel About Sex with Virgins," the responses from male interviewees seemed to say that when it comes to sex with virgins, guys feel ... conflicted. The responsibility they associate with that particular kind of encounter makes them unlikely to do it without certain parameters.

"If I were single, I'd probably have sex with a virgin. But only if we were dating. I'd be really uncomfortable being their first if we had met at a bar or something."

Another interviewee echoed the feeling: "Both times I slept with a virgin, it was in the context of a serious relationship. I really wouldn't do it any other way; otherwise you'd just be asking for trouble."[5]

Trouble? What kind of trouble? Do virgins who aren't in serious relationships grow fangs on their labia to destroy any non-committal penises that come their way?

I don't know if either of those men would have fallen into the gift category. Perhaps they did and that's what gave them a feeling of obligation to commit before sleeping with a virgin. But even men who make it clear that they don't subscribe to the gift theory of virginity ("I don't think virginity is magical!") are hesitant to have casual sex with a virgin because "if you have sex with a virgin, you're going to be part of [that] person's life story." I guess being a part of someone's life story is the opposite of casual.

Another article, this time published in the *Daily Californian*, featured a number of stories on the stigma of virginity from students participating in campus hookup culture. In one anecdote, a girl told the guy she was a virgin *after* they'd already had sex. "Had she told me that beforehand, I would have gotten the fuck out of there," he said.

And it isn't just men who are chiming in. Other women have plenty of stories similar to my experience with Kevin. (Although I've yet to hear of any other girl who had a guy climb a wall for her.) This one also comes from the *Daily Californian*: "I think he said this to me verbatim: 'I'm sorry, but you're just going to have to leave. It's not you. In my personal experience, girls who are virgins — after they have sex with a guy — they tend to be really clingy and won't leave him alone.'"[6]

This is a particularly problematic social trend because it reverts to giving the man all the control in the situation. Guys are anticipating how virgins are going to feel after having sex for the first time and are applying generalized stereotypes about female sexuality to all women who aren't yet sexually active. Furthermore, some of them even go so far as to act as if they know what's best for the woman. Since they don't want a commitment, or are just looking to have a casual fling, they tell themselves they're acting in the woman's best interests by not hooking up with someone who they believe will definitely get attached. This leaves no room for the personal agency of the female virgin to make her own choices about whether or not she wants to have a casual experience. It also negates the woman's freedom to manage her own emotions and choices around casual sex, all while perpetuating the negative stereotype of women as needy and clingy. The man, as the sexually experienced partner, claims to know what's best for both of them when it comes to the question of hooking up.

Still blissfully unaware of these dynamics, I woke up early the morning after the toga party. My cellphone had pinged and I could already hear my roommates starting the PGA in the kitchen. Text messages popped up on my screen and Kevin opened his eyes.

"Is there someone outside?" he asked.

I looked over and through the frosted glass panels of my bedroom door, I could clearly see a silhouette with her ear cocked toward us.

"Just ignore them," I said, and the shadow disappeared.

I lay in bed and answered my text messages from the girls downstairs (*"Is Kevin in our house!?!"*) while he dressed quickly. Despite how early it was, Kevin was already running late for his rehearsal. I sat up and looked at the floor. Something wasn't quite right.

"Are you wearing my socks?" I asked.

"What? Oh, shit!"

"You have tiny feet!"

"Yeah, yeah I do." He smiled. "Don't tell anyone."

We had a little secret to share.

Downstairs in the kitchen, we were greeted a little too enthusiastically by four women cradling their teacups. I stepped out the back door and onto the stoop with Kevin, hoping that the girls couldn't see us through gaps in the kitchen curtains. I expected him to kiss me goodbye. I don't remember exactly what we said, but it was some variation of:

"That was fun."

"Yeah. It was."

I looked up at him, tilting my chin toward him. He kissed me quickly. The kind of kiss I imagined a husband would give his wife before heading off to work in 1955.

That went relatively well.

I'd taken a big step forward and had gotten very close to accomplishing my goal pretty easily. I felt like the door was still open for us to hook up again in the future, but that the stars just hadn't quite aligned that evening. I had no idea that I was vastly underestimating the weight of my virgin baggage. Back inside, the girls launched into the usual morning-after questions, but for the first time they were directed at me.

"How did this happen?"

"What did you guys do?"

"Are you going to see him again?"

"How big is his penis?"

I told them what I could, but they were disappointed that I hadn't thought to measure his penis properly and, after giving me some specific instructions about how to do that secretly in the future, they thankfully didn't seem interested in discussing him any further.

I truly didn't know what would happen next. I thought he might call or text, but I knew there was also a good chance that wouldn't happen. We were just "hooking up," after all.

I thought we might go home from another party together sometime in the future, but the opportunity never arose again, and he never did pick up the phone. At least not to get in touch with me. Not much later, I saw him at a party with his arms around another girl and I knew it was time for me to look elsewhere.

A couple weeks after that, I tried to hook up with a friend of a friend who was visiting from another school. I'm not going to go into details, because nobody wants to read virtually the same series of events twice in one chapter. Guy comes home with me after a party, and we fool around. I use the same line to let him know where I'm at, but make it clear this time that I'm keen to move forward. The hands come off. We go to sleep; he leaves before breakfast; you can fill in the blanks.

I was starting to see a pattern.

At some point further on, Ellie told me that my name had come up in a conversation between her and Kevin after the toga party.

"He said you were nice," she told me. "Exactly that. Kevin said, 'Nellwyn is such a *nice* girl.'"

But I could tell there was something unspoken lingering on the end of his words. The same something that prompted him to take his hands off me and fall asleep when we weren't really tired at all.

CHAPTER 10

"IF YOU HAVEN'T HAD SEX by the end of the school year," one of my roommates said, "you can always have sex with Ethan."

I was sitting on the floor outside my bedroom with my back against the wall, tapping my toes together. Two of the girls were perched on the stairs in front of me, for some reason we'd decided that the landing outside my room was the best place to hunker down for some girl talk.

"Yeah, that's true," I said. "Or Ryan, maybe."

"No, don't waste your first time on Ryan," another of the girls said, speaking from experience.

I wasn't sure how seriously I should take her comment, but either way I thought it would be so much easier to have sex with Ethan.

Ethan had already had sex with both the girls sitting on the steps. He was the perfect "friend with benefits."

Ethan was basically one of the girls. He slept on our couch every other weekend and was often waiting for us downstairs the morning after a party, wrapped in a blanket and nursing a cup of tea, ready to start that day's Post-Game Analysis. He hung out with us when we had our hair piled up in messy topknots. He helped us make root beer floats on Tuesday nights and sang along with us as we rewatched our favourite childhood Disney films.

Ethan would have sex with both men and women, though he was more discreet about some of his hookups than others. Our understanding that he was likely still figuring out where he would fall on the fluid sexual spectrum kept him firmly in the no-strings-attached, friends-with-benefits, casual-hookup category.

The next weekend our friend Amy came over to pre-game before a major Halloween party. Her makeup was flawless and she'd highlighted her cheekbones to perfection. She stood in front of the bathroom mirror and fluffed up her short haircut while I curled my eyelashes painstakingly.

"If I don't hook up with anyone tonight, I'm just going to make out with Jim," she said, speaking about another one of our closest friends, who happened to be gay.

I laughed. "Yeah, me too."

"I mean, I just want to kiss *somebody* because I look amazing and I spent forever on this makeup. Otherwise, what's the point?"

"Hey, you don't need to tell me," I said. "Why else do you think I've made out with him at the last two parties?"

It seems strange now, but kissing Jim on a dance floor was like an extreme version of a high-five. It was more an extension of our friendship than it was truly sexual. And it made both of us feel better if we'd failed to get together with a boy we liked that evening. There was something so *safe* and comfortable about making out with someone you cared about, without any risk that you would fall in love.

I didn't have a costume for the Halloween party, so I raided every closet in the house and snaked my way into black leggings, a bodysuit, and skin-tight sparkly gold short-shorts. With oversized white socks and Mary Jane heels, I went to the party as an

American Apparel model. I made sure to tease my hair and lean up against walls a lot like the girls in the ads.

The party was like all the others. The same people. The same identical living rooms of the same identical townhouses we all lived in. The same DJs playing the same songs. I was trapped. Our campus was so isolated from the rest of the city that I figured I would almost definitely lose my virginity to one of the guys I had been partying with since I was eighteen. At least if I wanted to make Operation: Have Sex Before Twenty-First Birthday a success.

I wasn't surprised when Ethan kissed me. I was drunk. The only things I could feel were physical. What I could hear and touch and taste. Hip-hop and broad shoulders and gin on his lips. It was enough to get lost in the sea of being a popular party girl. As long as I had vodka and a man to dance with, I was satisfied. Ethan kissed me again and played with the hem of my shorts. My brain was so used to being fuzzy, to floating through the nights, to forgetting about anything that might hold me back that thoughts didn't exist. The only real things were the ones directly in front of me.

Ethan could have been a high-fashion model. Tall and lean, slightly androgynous, but thoroughly masculine all at once. Cheekbones to die for, piercing eyes, and soft, soft skin.

He went to get another drink and I busied myself with more leaning.

"Please let me go home with him." A desperate voice behind me seemed aimed in my direction.

I turned around and there was Ashley. A girl a year below me who I'd heard had slept with Ethan a couple times.

"What?" I squinted and grimaced, shocked that she had even thought to say something like that.

"I know you're going to go home with him. But please don't. Please let him go home with me."

"He can go home with whoever he wants." I shrugged as if I didn't care one way or the other.

Ashley had just broken up with her boyfriend and she needed someone to grab on to. Something solid to hold in the dizzy haze of alcohol and cigarettes. Something that felt real, but would disappear in the morning. The problem was that I needed the same thing.

Ethan ended up going home with me, though we were too tired and drunk to do anything but fall asleep. A year before, I would have felt like I'd won. I would have luxuriated in that simple, shallow validation, but even that feeling was starting to dim. I needed more.

I suppose that's why I agreed to be Ethan's girlfriend when he asked me, knowing that we could never be in a real relationship. I suspected that Ethan still had a lot to figure out about his sexual and romantic life, and if I'd been less selfish or less hurt, I wouldn't have gotten involved with him at all. I knew our relationship wouldn't last. I wasn't in it to last. I was in it so that I could come to my next boyfriend minus one very heavy piece of virgin baggage.

For our first real "date," Ethan offered to cook me dinner. He showed up with arms full of grocery bags and together in the kitchen we made pasta while my roommates listened in from the living room. He brought candles for the dining-room table and lit them while I poured the red wine.

"This feels very fancy," I said.

"Well, isn't that what you do on dates?" he replied.

I went through the motions. We sat on the same side of the kitchen table. I drank deep sips from my glass of wine and twirled my spaghetti delicately around and around and around my fork. I crossed my legs and leaned in and wore the sexy underwear.

But at the end of the night, Ethan packed up his candles and went home. Yet again, a man who'd slept with countless other women declined to sleep with me. I told myself he was just being first-date chivalrous.

"You're exactly his type of girl," my roommates said. "He always does this. He finds a sweet pretty girl who likes to read and puts her on a pedestal."

I didn't care. I'd balance myself on that pedestal as long as I could get what I wanted, too. I figured our relationship had a shelf life of about a month. Six weeks, tops.

I went to the next party with a new sense of security. There's something to be said for knowing who you're going home with. Knowing you'll have someone to talk to on your walk home, someone to remind you to drink two glasses of water before bed, someone to share your second pillow with.

Ethan kissed me on the dance floor with his mouth open. Wide kisses with lots of air between them.

Then he disappeared.

I must have thought he'd gone to get another drink, but when he didn't come back, I started to feel out of place, like my hands were too big for my body. When I'd been single, I'd never felt alone at a party. There were almost always boys to dance with and when there weren't, there were girls. But in that moment all my girl-friends had coupled up and suddenly it was no longer acceptable for me to throw myself at the nearest guy. Desperate to never again be a wallflower, I went searching for Ethan.

I found him on the other side of the building, pacing back and forth around a big empty room.

"You're avoiding me," I said.

The anguish in his face was Shakespearean.

"I know." His voice echoed.

I leaned against a table and crossed my arms.

"Pretty dick move," I said casually.

"I have to break up with you," he blurted out. The corners of his mouth pointed down toward the floor. "I think I'm gay. I mean, I *am* gay."

"Okay." I nodded and smiled encouragingly.

Perhaps he'd expected a more dramatic response to coming out of the closet, but I was trying to normalize his experience and show him that his sexuality didn't change anything about him or our friendship.

"You're not upset?" His eyes narrowed.

"No," I said honestly. "If you're gay, you're gay."

That seemed to trigger something lingering in the back of his mind.

"Oh my god," he shouted at the ceiling. "How am I going to tell my dad?"

He started fumbling with the pockets of his coat, looking for his iPhone.

"I have to tell my dad," he panicked. "I have to call my dad right now."

Ethan's father had moved to Canada from a country not well known for its acceptance of homosexuality.

"Ethan." I stood up from my perch against the table and moved toward him. "I don't think this is the best time —"

"Hello?" Ethan must have had his parents on speed dial. "Hi — Jamie —"

His older brother had answered the 2:00 a.m. phone call. Ethan started to cry. Tears were rolling slowly down his face, but he kept his voice steady.

"I'm okay," he said. "I just — I don't know what to do. I've been seeing this girl and —"

He kept rubbing his eyes.

"Ethan," I said, "hang up the phone. You're drunk."

"— it's just not working," he continued. "And it made me realize, I have to tell you. I'm pretty sure I'm gay."

Silence finally settled over the room. Minutes passed. His brother seemed to have a lot more to say on the subject than I did.

Finally, Ethan pulled the phone away from his ear and held it out toward me.

"He wants to talk to you," he said.

"What?" I whispered. "This has nothing to do with me! What am I supposed to say?"

"Just talk to him. Please." He shoved the phone in my hands.

"Hi, Jamie." I stared up at the ceiling, praying for a lightning bolt to obliterate me.

"Hey. So you're my brother's girlfriend."

"Well, no …" I let the word drag and wondered if I was being too pedantic. Alcohol tends to make me too picky about certain things.

"He said you were his girlfriend." Jamie's voice was deep and firm.

"Well, he just told me he's gay," I said. "So no, I'm not his girlfriend.... Anymore."

"Okay, but like — as his girlfriend — do you think he's gay?"

I breathed in and counted to three.

"I think he's gay if he says he's gay."

"But, like." Jamie paused for only a second. "How gay do you think he actually is?"

"I really think you should talk to your brother."

"But, I mean, you've been dating him, so you would know if he's gay —"

I don't remember exactly how many times we went around in circles, but by the end Ethan was lying on the floor, covering his face with his arms and crying.

"Look," I said in my most authoritative twenty-year-old voice. "He's really upset, and he's very, very drunk. Right now my only concern is getting him home in one piece. Call him in the morning."

I hung up the phone and threw it in my purse.

"Come on, Ethan, we're going home."

"No!" He tightened his arms around his head as if they would keep him locked in place. "I can't move."

"Get up." I tried to be nice and authoritative all at the same time. "I understand this is a big day for you, but you're not sleeping here. I'm taking you home."

"I'm not worthy …" He began to wail.

Not worthy. Not worthy of what?

"Yes, you are, you can get up now." I tugged on his elbow and half-dragged him to his feet.

"All right," I said. "Now we're going to walk to my place, and you're going to drink two glasses of water and sleep on the futon."

"No! No, I can't."

"Okay, that's fine, then I'll walk you to your place. Let's go," I coaxed.

We slipped out a back door into the early winter night, avoiding going back into the party. Ethan's phone in my bag kept ringing. I saw his brother's name on the call display through the open zipper.

"Is that my phone?" he asked.

"No, it's mine," I lied, turning off the volume. "Don't worry, I'll call them back."

Ethan dipped back and forth across the sidewalk, weaving from one side to the other. I couldn't hold him. He wouldn't let me guide him.

"I can't go home," he wailed again. "Don't walk with me, just leave me here."

Ethan flung himself into the gutter on the side of the road.

"I'm going to sleep here," he shouted. "I'm not worthy."

What was underneath this *cri de coeur*? What had we accidentally done to each other?

"It's okay," I said. "Yes, you are. You're not sleeping here. Everything is going to be okay. You just have to get up and walk."

I tried and tried in my most reassuring tone until I realized I wasn't getting anywhere. Standing in the cold, when I spoke again my voice was harsh. Too sharp for my own good. "You are going to get up and *walk*. You are not a child. Get. Up."

Dragging his heels, he subdued his sobbing. Hiccupping occasionally, he finally let me walk him home. I made sure he made it through his front door before turning around and walking home alone, disappointed, but not at all surprised.

The next morning, he showed up at my front door. No one ever used our front door. Everyone except the postman knew to come in through the backyard. I'd never seen Ethan at the front door in our entire friendship.

"I need to talk to you," he said, standing on the front stoop.

"I don't think there's anything else to say." I wasn't at all angry, I was tired.

"Please."

I opened the door and let him follow me in.

"I need to talk to you about what I said last night," he said.

"Okay."

"I told you some stuff … but the truth is that I'm not gay." He looked at me somewhat sheepishly. "I just wanted to break up with you and didn't know how to tell you."

"Okay."

"That's all you have to say?"

"Yeah," I said. I was firmly opting out of his identity crisis, and I felt truly emotionless about the whole thing.

"Aren't you upset?" he asked.

I honestly wasn't. "Ethan, it sounds like you have a lot of stuff to work through, and I think you should go do that. So, no, I'm not upset."

"But I don't have anything to work through. I'm not gay."

"Okay."

"I'm not!"

"Okay," I said, standing up. "I'll see you later."

After that day, Ethan went back to sleeping with women publicly and men secretly. Or so he thought, but the men he slept with gossiped as much as we did. He slept with my roommates again, he slept with Ashley again, but he never slept with me.

·   ·   •   ·   ·

I know we hooked up with gay men because it was more fun than hooking up with no one. At the time we thought it was easy, harmless, no-strings-attached fun. The ultimate friends with benefits. I've heard of women who accidentally fall in love with their gay friends, but that was never a risk for any of us. Making out with a gay man was something to laugh about with him the next morning. Proof of just how close your friendship with him really was.

"Oh my god, Jim, did we make out last night?"

"Ha-ha-ha yeah! We totally did!"

"High-five!"

Years later, I wondered if this post-postmodern gender-fluid model of campus hookups was a unique experience of ours that I should simply chalk up to having gone to art school. Maybe I could shrug the whole thing off as an aspect of being a free-spirited theatre student who spent a good portion of instructional class time meditating.

But now I know we weren't that special. We're talking about broader social trends here, and I wasn't the only girl caught in the crosshairs.

Kristina and her gay best friend Nick had a sexual relationship in college just like the ones my friends had with Ethan, and that I was trying to emulate. As I learned about her story, a few sentences jumped out at me as if I was reading my own diary from my undergraduate days.

"We used to make out on dance floors to try and incite jealousy in the boys we liked.

"I had been with someone I cared about and felt comfortable with and there was none of the usual dread associated with hetero-sexual friend hookups.

"At that time in my life it seemed like if I didn't find someone to go home with or make out with, my night was a failure."[1]

Bingo!

It wasn't hard at all to find other stories that seemed very similar to mine. On a women's lifestyle website, *The Frisky,* an anonymous writer tells the story of her ongoing friends-with-benefits relation-ship with her gay friend Adam. "For me, this was fun and games, a way to have great sex with someone I loved, but without the com-plications of an actual relationship. And I will be the first to admit it, it was the ultimate ego boost. This is a guy who wasn't sexually attracted to women, and yet he was *very* attracted to me. I was so freaking hot that I turned a gay man straight!"

There it is. The one thing none of my friends or I ever said out loud.

Another form of questionable validation.

What we didn't stop to think about at the time was how we were yet again boosting our self-esteem through our sexual encounters with men. And it wasn't until Ethan's breakdown that I realized the emotional stakes may have been higher for him than I had thought.

I realize that, to many people, these cross-orientation experi-ences might be surprising, but we were taking the first steps toward a new and still developing era of sexual experimentation and acceptance. An era where gender and orientation are more openly fluid than ever before.

There are entire subsets of scholars who study this phenome-non. What they call "mixed-orientation relationships" is a term I learned from Dr. Francesca Gaiba, professor and associate director at Northwestern University's Institute for Sexual and Gender Minority Health and Wellbeing. Her work is peppered with even more stories that seem all too familiar ...

One of Dr. Gaiba's interviewees describes a gay male friend of hers who, despite being in his early forties at the time of the interview, reminded me of Ethan: "He is right now struggling ... because I think he has wanted to believe for a long time that he is bisexual or might wind up being heterosexual. But finds over time that his real attraction is almost always to men."

Dr. Gaiba goes on to explain that this man had frequent anonymous sex with men, but never settled into an openly gay relationship. Ethan, too, slept with gay men quietly and secretly (or so he thought), but made a point to present a straight identity in public.

The trouble is that we have placed too much emphasis on sexual orientation as a character-defining quality. Though we are slowly beginning to better understand and accept sexual fluidity, there is an established idea that sexual orientation is always fixed and unchangeable. Not only does that orientation then become a key part of your identity, it also dictates your behaviour. If you're a gay man, you sleep with men. If you're a straight man, you sleep with women. Full stop. No arguments. As Dr. Gaiba writes, "Once an identity is adopted, one is expected to behave accordingly in future interactions."[2]

Instead of relying on sexual behaviour to construct so much of our core identities, Dr. Gaiba presents a constructivist approach which argues that "sexual identity is not a static representation of essential being, but a dynamic description of the self in relation to others." Meaning that it can be changeable and subject to the uniqueness of individual experiences. Sexual behaviour does not have to dictate immutable personal identity.

Ethan's emotional breakdown that night at the party came in part from an identity crisis piqued by his coming out. I keep thinking of his words, "I'm not worthy." Where did they come from? They speak to something more and greater than a desire to have sex with men; they reflect how this desire made Ethan feel about who he was in his very core. In those moments, he was a casualty of a society that has placed too much emphasis on a person's sex life as a core piece of one's personal identity.

· · ● · ·

A year after my "relationship" with Ethan, he had to write and perform a monologue on the topic of his choice for a class assignment. Ethan stood up in front of our professors and fellow students and spoke for seven minutes about the girl he loved. The girl he was incapable of loving. The reasons he was not worthy.

That weekend he asked me to dance at a party.

"My monologue was about you," he said. "I love you."

Ethan loved the idea of me. The sweet, virginal girl who would probably make a really good girlfriend. The girl he wanted to want.

CHAPTER 11

WHEN I SAW HIM IN PRAGUE, Jake was walking away from me or sitting halfway across the bar, something like that. Either way, he didn't notice me, and I remember thinking, *Oh, he's here. That makes sense.*

I lived with five girls in a one-bedroom apartment in Prague for two weeks in the summer of 2011. We roamed the museums by day and the five-storey dance clubs by night. Everything we owned fit in our brand-new backpacks and every day ended with a two-dollar pint.

About twenty-five students from our school had taken over the city to volunteer at the Prague Quadrennial, the world's largest festival devoted to performance design. We also got to meet theatre students from around the world, which came in very handy in the weeks after the festival.

Travel Tip #1: Make local friends early on so you can always get a drink at 5:00 a.m.

Jake was in theatre school with me in Toronto, so I wasn't surprised to see him hanging around with other fellow classmates in Prague. We were in the same year, but we didn't have any classes in common since he was in the acting program and I was in play-writing. He lived with his parents off-campus and didn't party much, so we'd never gotten to know each other. I guess I have to confess I'd sort of forgotten he existed until I saw him in the Czech Republic.

Crossing the road near the Charles Bridge on one of my first afternoons in the city, I got excited about the possibility of meeting a European man. Europeans are inherently sexy. Why? Maybe because they drink wine before 5:00 p.m. and live surrounded by art and architecture and beauty. Maybe because the men aren't afraid to use hair product and buy expensive shoes.

But here's the problem: Europeans don't dance like we do.

When I was thirteen, my cousin Brooke came along on a family road trip from Niagara Falls to Saskatoon. That road trip, if you drive through Canada like we did, is 3,063 kilometres, 1,903.26 miles, or thirty-two hours long.

Travel Tip #2: Don't drive from Niagara Falls to Saskatoon with four teenagers.

Somewhere in middle-of-nowhere-Canada, we pulled our green minivan into a rest stop for lunch. Tired of looking at identical stretches of prairie highway, Brooke and I snuck around back to hang out by the Dumpsters.

"I learned how to pole-dance," Brooke said, making it sound like pole-dancing was something every woman should know how to do.

"Can you teach me?"

She began moving her hips back and forth, making little circles and figure eights in the air. I watched and tried to copy her.

"No. Don't move your knees," she said. "Move *just* your hips."

That's what I thought I was doing.

"Stop moving your knees. Think sexy."

I gave up.

This all came rushing back to me a few years later when I started partying. Turns out that dancing is the same as pole-dancing. In North America at least. Despite my rocky start, I picked up dancing pretty easily once I got a little older and a little more self-confident. Brooke was right: all you really have to know how to do is move your hips as if they're independent from the rest of your body. Maybe move your shoulders every once in a while to show off the bronzer you dusted on your cleavage. And if you find a dance partner, things are still pretty straightforward: simply move your hips up against his (or hers!) instead of in thin air. Turn around once in a while and grind back-to-front so that you can avoid the awkwardness of actually having to look your partner in the eye. This is the only way I've ever seen Canadian girls dance at a party.

On our second-last night in Prague, the festival threw a party for all the students who'd come to volunteer. By this time, we were starting to get the idea that we weren't really fitting in on the European dance floors. What we were up against was something closer to *interpretive* dance. These girls were imagining they were a melting candle, or a feather on a breeze, or a piece of flotsam in the waves. And they were *working it.*

There was no way we could keep up. We weren't groomed to consider dancing at parties as a form of artistic expression: we considered it a form of foreplay.

The party was on the second floor of festival headquarters. We bypassed the offices where we'd worked for the last two weeks and climbed a barren staircase. The room was dark and glowed faintly purple. Weak beams of light from the street threatened, but never quite managed, to break through the windows along the far wall. Music pumped in from somewhere, but I don't remember a DJ. The bar was a collapsible conference room table, but inviting cans of beer and little plastic cups of wine were lined up along it.

It seemed everyone was there. All the students we'd met over the last two weeks were hitting the dance floor and bringing their internal movement-metaphors with them. My group of five Canadians hovered by the door.

"Ugh. *More* European dancing."

I grabbed a drink off the table and made my way over to a window. At least they were playing music with a strong beat. North American girls know what to do with a strong beat. We were never going to be the girls at the party who danced barefoot wearing a daisy-chain, so we did what we knew how to do. We started moving our hips. Somewhere across the room I caught some Europeans giving us funny looks. I chose to ignore them.

"How come we've never hung out before this?"

I turned around. It was Jake.

"I don't know. Must be coincidence."

"We've been in the same program for three years and we've never hung out."

"Sorry …"

What did he want from me? Was I supposed to feel guilty because he didn't party? It's not like he wasn't invited, and he had certainly never invited me to hang out before.

The music started to take an even sexier turn. He didn't say anything.

"It's just — well, I never see you at parties," I continued.

"I live kind of far."

"Oh. Well, we're hanging out now, aren't we?"

We drank a few more beers and the music took a really North American turn with one of my all-time least favourite songs: "I Just Had Sex."

"I just had seeeexx," Jake started singing along. "And it felt so gooood."

He sang so enthusiastically it made me wonder if he'd lost his virginity sometime in the last twenty-four hours. I didn't think it was really plausible. He was a little bit older, and besides, I was pretty sure I was the only virgin left in the world. But he seemed a little too keen to sing his sexual prowess to the world. I winced a little and sipped my beer.

Watching him sing along reminded me of what it's like to be seventeen, and something about the whole scene was so silly it almost seemed endearing. After all, didn't every one of us feel like we had something to prove? Our sex lives were synonymous with our identities; maybe he needed to feel like a man, but it just made him seem insecure about sex. You know what they say about over-confident men: if he drives a red convertible sports car with a spoiler and satellite radio, he's probably insecure about the size of his penis. It's Overcompensation 101.

As much as I might joke about the sports cars, it must be hard to be a man in a culture that has as fucked-up ideas about masculinity as it does about femininity. In an article on a men's interest website, sexologist Dr. Hernando Chaves writes about the connection between expectations of masculinity and sexual anxiety:

> Maybe our anxiety around sex comes from the expectations imposed on masculinity in our culture, from watching porn, from our depictions of how men act in the media, from fears or insecurities that fuel this need to perform. It could be because of our desire for partner or peer validation that we think we need to excel in something that every man is supposed to be a stud at doing.[1]

In Jake's case, maybe it was just the beer.

By now we were dancing together and I was the one wondering why on earth we hadn't ever hung out before. He was good-looking in an unconventional way and there was something beautifully unabashed about him. Honest. Confident. I told myself that he was just singing because he was drunk and liked to sing. He took me by the hips, I wrapped my arms around his neck and we were dancing together enthusiastically. The North American way.

Somewhere in the background I could hear people laughing at us, but I didn't care. They could keep their artistic expression. I was really starting to *like* this guy.

The party ended early and students were lined up outside the ice cream parlour next door by the time we found ourselves in the street. Instead of joining the crowd, Jake and I turned left and walked toward the river. We turned another corner and the Gothic towers of the Charles Bridge rose up ahead of us. In the early morning light, it was a shadow against the deep dark blue-black sky. The lamps all along both sides of the bridge were lit up to guide midnight strollers over the water, but its wide stone walkway was quiet and deserted. Jake held my hand as we wandered halfway across and stopped to take in the view. The barriers over the river were low and they dug into my stomach as I leaned over. It began to rain softly and the bridge started to smell wet. Fresh and old at the same time. I could hear the rain hitting all the stones and trickling into the cracks between them. As it fell into the river, it made a brighter sound. The banks started to get muddy and the brown smell of freshly made mud rose up high above to where we stood in the middle of the bridge. The lights blurred and my hair started to stick to my neck and my forehead. My vision seemed foggy through the rain.

Every once in a while, soft footsteps approached, passed us by, and disappeared again as some other night owl crossed from one side of the city to the other. No one spoke and we felt compelled to whisper. The Prague Castle was lit up far in the distance at the top of a hill on the west bank of the river. Its Gothic towers glowed, painting a far more beautiful picture of the city than the Hollywood-style sign behind us that screamed in bold white letters: THE TEARS OF STALIN.

Despite the lanterns guiding the way across the Vltava River, somehow we could still see all the stars. I looked for Orion like I always do, but couldn't find him. I started to shiver and Jake put his arms around me. Our skin was damp from the summer rain, but neither one of us wanted to move.

He told me about his family, his upcoming travels, his secret ambitions for his career.

"When do you leave?" he asked.

"The day after tomorrow. You?"

"Same."

He paused.

"I wanted to climb that mountain before I left," he said. "The one with the funicular."

He was talking about Petrin Hill, a park that rose high above the bank of the river where we were standing.

"Why don't you?" I asked.

"I didn't have time."

"Well, you could climb it tomorrow," I suggested.

"Only if you come with me."

I didn't particularly want to hike up a mountain on a hot summer day, but Petrin Hill was pretty much the only tourist attraction in Prague I hadn't seen. And he had his arms around me.

"Yes," I said, smiling. "Let's climb the mountain."

• • • • •

We spent our last afternoon in Prague bypassing the funicular and climbing our way to the very top of Petrin Hill. We collapsed on the grass side by side to bask in our accomplishment under the blinding sun. I wiped the sweat off my forehead and prayed that my hair hadn't gone too frizzy. Beyond the green parks, the terracotta-coloured roofs of the city stretched out for miles until they became nothing more than orange blurs melting into the horizon. I lay back in the grass and closed my eyes.

"I'm glad we got to do this," I said.

"Where are you going next?" he asked.

"Berlin. Then Brussels, Bruges, Luxembourg, Amsterdam, and London. You?"

"Italy, mostly. When are you home?"

"Early August," I replied.

"Me too."

"Well, you'll have to start coming to parties now, won't you?"

Travel Tip #3: Never fall for a guy in the first city you visit. It puts a damper on the rest of the trip.

• • • •

Weeks later, back on Canadian soil, we started dating enthusiastically. He surprised me with concert tickets and carried a bottle of wine around secretly all evening so that we could enjoy a clandestine glass in the harbour looking out over Lake Ontario. He took me to his favourite restaurants, insisted I order generous portions, and took care of the bill on the sly. He picked me up in his car and caressed my hand as we waited for the lights to turn from red to green. He introduced me to his friends from high school who were "so happy to meet me" and had "heard so much about me." I fell asleep on the subway with my head on his shoulder.

But he never came home with me at the end of the night.

The closest we got to being in bed together was when we went window-shopping at IKEA after mistaking the movie times at the theatre next door. Jake was strong but he spoke quietly and tucked in his shoulders so they looked smaller. I didn't realize how strong he was until he sat down next to me in the IKEA showroom and reached his arm across the back of the sofa to pull me in close. He didn't care that we were in the middle of a crowded store. He held me tightly and ran his thumb up and down my arm, pretending this was our private living room. Our home.

I was uncomfortable doing something so intimate in public, so I got up and moved through the showrooms. Next came the bedrooms. He followed behind me and guided us both down onto a twin bed with white sheets. I heard the plastic price tags crackling beneath us. We lay down and he whispered in my ear and I could feel the eyes of every bargain furniture shopper in the North York IKEA staring at us. He didn't seem to notice. He didn't seem to care.

When our school and rehearsal schedules soon made it impossible for us to go on normal dates, he would wake up early and drive to campus to take me out for breakfast before my 8:30 a.m. class. You can see why it was easy to like him, but after four months of regular dating and almost six months since we'd started cyber-flirting our way through Europe, something wasn't right. He had still never once stepped foot inside my house. He had never even tried to make it past the front steps. I thought he was too old-fashioned for his own good.

One day in late autumn, we met for breakfast at the campus diner for our usual early morning date. I remember the world was orange. Orange morning sky, orange leaves, orange lights overhead. Silence fell over our greasy eggs and Wonder Bread toast. It lingered. I dumped all the creamers out of the little bowl and started stacking them as high as they would go. I took sugar packets and plastic stir-sticks and added them to my sculpture.

"It's art," I said.

He joined in. We knocked our sculpture over and started again. We built cream and sugar artwork without having anything else to say. I wondered why he'd never tried to touch me. I mean *really* touch me. I felt like we were running out of time. Our relationship was expiring before my eyes but I thought about the Charles Bridge and I remembered the Prague city skyline at night reflected in the river, and I wasn't ready to give up. I had waited too long for this. But then again, your boyfriend shouldn't be the person who makes you feel undesirable.

Back then I believed in the Myth of Men, and it tormented me. The Myth of Men is that "they are always supposed to be arousable, willing, and able to partake in sex."[2] I believed that. The myth had caught me hook, line, and sinker, which meant that the longer Jake waited to take me to bed, the more undesirable I thought I was. If a man didn't want sex, it was obviously because there was something wrong with *me*.

We all remember the seminal phrase: *he's just not that into you*. I first heard it when I was twelve or thirteen and watching *Sex and the City* for the first time. It was in reruns by then and was airing on regular television with the particularly steamy bits edited out. In one memorable episode, Carrie's boyfriend Jack Berger weighs in on some girl talk and offers her friend Miranda some life-changing advice about men:

MIRANDA: So he kissed me good night at the door. I invited him up, he couldn't because he had an early meeting. We kissed again. Then he said he'd call.
[...]
BERGER: All right. I'm not gonna sugar-coat it for you. He's just not that into you.... Look, I'm sorry but when a guy's really into you, he's coming upstairs, meeting or no meeting.

That advice made sense to me at the time, and I learned early on that men only have one level. Now, as I write this, I'm trying to figure out if that idea is more damaging to women or to men. Either way, it's pretty fucked up. The idea that men don't have feelings or concerns or extenuating circumstances beyond the surface was further propagated when the book *He's Just Not That Into You* came out a year later. The book's premise centres on the idea that if a man isn't making the effort to pursue you — sexually or otherwise — he's just not that into you. The book made it to the *New York Times* bestseller list with sales of more than 1.5 million copies, was featured on *Oprah*, and was adapted into a 2009 film featuring a star-studded cast.

Sometimes I think we're all totally fucked.

Berger's advice to Miranda was meant to be liberating: stop wasting your time on guys who can't see how fabulous you really are! But the truth is that it has fostered a generation of women who are quick to throw a boyfriend out with the bongwater. At the same time, the idea dehumanizes men as one-dimensional sex machines and leaves no room for the nuances of individual human experience.

Culture writer Ramin Setoodeh said it perfectly in a *Newsweek* article that appeared in 2009 shortly after the release of the film:

> The "Not Into You" thesis is less about offering any insights into relationships, and more about embracing laziness. It takes advantage of this generation's collective impatience.... Technology has made it easier to meet new people (MySpace, Facebook) but also to write them off, via text message. If the messages are too muddled, "Not Into You" has the easy fix: find somebody else. Because the options are limitless, nobody is really worth the trouble.[3]

Thank you, Ramin, can I buy you a drink? I want to toast your brilliant critique, but I also want to discuss my other concern: the socially pervasive idea that men don't have mixed feelings, deep emotions, or brains capable of processing anything other than "Must. Procreate. Now."

The "Not Into You" theory fails men because it perpetuates the myth that men are nothing more than sexual automatons. That manhood is attached to a particular type of sexual prowess and that having doubts, fears, or emotions of any kind is failing at a crucial aspect of man-ness.

The "Not Into You" theory fails women because it teaches that a woman's desirability is inherently linked to whether or not a man takes her home. If there are never any extenuating circumstances for a man to call it an early night, and if men are always in pursuit of sex, the only reason he could have for leaving you at your front door is that he doesn't want you. Not now, not *ever*. The terrible conclusion is that you are undesirable in some way. Since straight women are taught the importance of attracting men from an incredibly young age (why else do you think I was watching *Sex and the City* at twelve years old?), this means that we have failed at a crucial aspect of woman-ness.

Back in 2011, I hadn't figured all this out yet. I sat at breakfast, making sculptures out of mini-milk cartons instead of making real conversation because I couldn't process a boyfriend who seemed to want me so much in the day and so little at night.

Jake mentioned he loved *South Park*.

"I've never seen it," I said.

"Not even the movie?"

"Nope. Never."

I balanced another creamer upside down on top of the pile.

"Maybe we should watch it together," I suggested. "You could come over to my place."

"It's a date."

Everyone knows that *Come over and watch a movie* is universal code for *Come over and have sex.* This was the night.

It wasn't too late, after all.

It's important, when you know *tonight* is *the* night, that you don't *look* like you know anything at all. I got ready for this casual stay-at-home date the same way I would get ready for a blow-out bash. Black underwear. Lace trim. Shaved legs. But I went for subtle makeup and brushed my hair so it hung long and soft and simple around my shoulders. I put on my best jeans and a cozy-but-stylish grey sweater. I was rocking "The Girl Next Door." I had absolutely no desire to watch the *South Park* movie. I was secretly hoping we would get "distracted" no more than thirty minutes in.

He showed up on my front steps with a smile. It was a perfect autumn day, and this was the life I used to dream about when I was sixteen and alone. Instead of taking him into the living room where we kept our shared TV, I led him straight upstairs to my tiny bedroom. It was easy to make up some excuse for wanting privacy, I lived with six other girls, after all. I set my computer up on my nightstand so we could sit together on the bed. I planned to get "tired" early on and find myself conveniently horizontal.

The gratuitous noise that is *South Park: Bigger, Longer & Uncut* droned on and on and I tried to remember to at least smirk a little bit whenever he laughed. I started mentally calculating how much time could possibly be left and tried not to look bored. That's something guys used to tell me: "You look bored." I guess you're not supposed to think critically in front of men, it makes you look uninterested.

It wasn't until after the credits had started to roll that he kissed me. Thanks to my careful planning, we were already lying together on the bed, our bodies touching. *Come over and watch a movie.* It never fails.

"Just so you know," I said, echoing myself, "I'm a virgin."

My clothes were already half off when I felt it: my moral compass demanding honesty. I knew I had to tell him, but I didn't think it would be a big deal this time. He was no one-night stand; we were in a relationship. This was November. If you counted our adventures in Prague, we'd been dating for nearly six months, and he'd never even put his hands under my shirt.

"Oh." He paused. "Are you sure you want to do this?"

"Yes. Very."

I let him take the lead and I felt like the pressure was off. It was dark outside by now and no light could make its way into my room from the street. My windows faced the brick wall of the house next door only three feet away. I reached over and turned off the light on my nightstand. He exhaled and I thought I heard the sound of disappointment under his breath, but I ignored it completely. I kept doing what I knew I was good at already and waited for him to initiate the next step. I didn't really know how to do it myself and I wanted to be led by someone who knew more than I did.

But nothing was happening.

That day, the Myth of Men told me I was ugly, naive, prudish, and boring. Today, research tells me that erectile difficulties are *extremely* common, though rarely spoken about. One recent study found that 43 percent of two thousand men surveyed were afflicted in some way, with 40 percent citing stress and 30 percent citing anxiety as the suspected causes.[4]

I am here now to debunk the Myth of Men, with a little help from our friendly neighbourhood therapist, Larry O'Connor.

Possibly every man will suffer from sexual performance anxiety at one time or another during the course of his sexual life. Sexual performance anxiety occurs when a man anticipates having some form of difficulty, such as difficulties with, or maintaining erections, or lack of arousal, causing him to be anxious or even panicked approaching or during sex. This can lead to a lack of desire, or an avoidance of sex all together.[5]

Similar ideas are echoed widely by other experts, but even the language we use to talk about male "performance" anxiety is inherently flawed. Thinking about sex in these terms establishes it as an act to be perfected, scrutinized, and critiqued, casting the person who should be your partner as the audience for whom you must perform. As the National Social Anxiety Center puts it, "This performance mindset leads many men to be self-conscious, self-critical, worried, tense, and anxious while being sexual. This in turn often results in bringing about the very problem they were worrying about in the first place."[6]

This is what I needed to hear. I needed someone to tell me it wasn't my fault. I needed someone to explain that I am not responsible for, or capable of guaranteeing, anyone's erection.

At a dinner party in my mid-twenties, I was surprised when a friend of a friend casually started talking about Viagra over cocktails. He seemed to have no qualms admitting that he kept a stash on hand to help him overcome first-time jitters with a new partner. In his early thirties, this man had no medical issues, serious psychological hang-ups, or age-related erectile dysfunction. He was also far from being sexually or romantically inexperienced. He spoke about the nerves and the pressure he felt when sleeping with someone for the first time, particularly someone he liked and wanted to continue to date. He turned to the other guys in the group for acknowledgement and recognition, a shared male understanding. Many in the group nodded subtly and agreed, though no one else had tried a pharmaceutical approach.

A man I interviewed not long after also confessed how much his nerves and emotions had occasionally impacted his romantic life and made it impossible for him to have sex with a woman he deeply cared for the first time they went to bed together.

"It's so frustrating. It's the worst. It's the worst feeling I think I've ever had.... If I could just say 'let's go' and it would happen, then it would happen. But it's not something that you can just make happen with your mind. It's out of your hands."

Another interviewee who agreed to be quoted on the condition that I only refer to him as E.D. made a strong connection between sexual performance anxiety and emotional vulnerability. He spoke about how, when the emotional stakes are high with a woman, that's when there is potential for bumps in the road. When it came to casual hookups and one-night stands, there was never a problem. Instead, emotional vulnerability caused greater anxiety and a stronger desire to please his partner, combined with the corresponding pressures and fears that come with that desire to please.

"Viagra doesn't remove emotional vulnerability," he told me. "Emotional intimacy becomes more accessible when performance anxiety is eliminated. A potential obstacle has been erased."

The omnipresent fear of not being able to live up to the occasion, which can itself derail a sexual encounter, is also emphasized by therapist Larry O'Connor:

> Given the importance of sex — biologically, emotionally, and socially for men, the fear of not being able to perform is always present if even to varying degrees, causing problems of confidence in and out of the bedroom.[7]

That's another thing I needed to hear: "The fear of not being able to perform is *always* present." If I'd known, maybe I would have understood, maybe I would have been more patient, maybe I wouldn't have felt so unattractive.

Pharmaceuticals aren't necessarily the answer. While they can be a great solution for people who genuinely need them, I worry about the idea that they are being used when not medically necessary, like in the case of my friend at the dinner party. In non-medical cases, they're being used as a Band-Aid that conceals and perpetuates the real problem: we've overvalued sexual virility and left little room for men to be emotionally vulnerable, nervous, or insecure. Stories that counter this narrative are important in terms of reframing how we, as a culture, generalize, stereotype, and think about male sexual desire, virility, and so-called performance.

· · • · ·

Back in my bedroom with Jake, we were at a standstill.

"Maybe this is for the best," he said. "If it was really going to be your first time and everything ..."

Like Kevin, he slept over as if we were the perfect couple I'd always dreamt about. He had to leave early in the morning, so he kissed me goodbye in the kitchen and promised to talk to me soon. I knew then that our relationship would never be anything close to what I wanted it to be. I would never feel beautiful when I saw my face reflected in his eyes; I was convinced he didn't really want me.

The Myth of Men had won another battle, and I was slowly losing the war.

CHAPTER 12

I MET BEN WHEN a beautiful and incredibly badass stranger moved in next door. My new neighbour was from New York City, had a super chic haircut, and seemed to epitomize the Cool Girl archetype.

I'll never forget the day I learned about the Cool Girl. I was reading Gillian Flynn's novel *Gone Girl* and was struck by a passage that has since become famous in feminist circles. This paragraph suddenly gave me the perfect definition of what I had been trying to achieve all my life.

Being the Cool Girl means I am a hot, brilliant, funny woman who adores football, poker, dirty jokes, and burping, who plays video games, drinks cheap beer, loves threesomes and anal sex, and jams hot dogs and hamburgers into her mouth like she's hosting the world's biggest culinary gang bang while somehow maintaining a size 2, because Cool Girls are above all hot.[1]

At first I thought, *Yes! This is exactly the male-centric ideal I've felt pressured to emulate all my life.*

And then I thought, *But I actually* do *like beer and poker. I* am *a size two and I once ate five hamburgers in one week. Because I love hamburgers.*

I wondered if I really do like all these things or if I learned to like them because, subconsciously, I knew it would make me the Cool Girl, and I know that's who every man wants to date. But then again: who *doesn't* love hamburgers?

Whether she intended to or not, my new neighbour had mastered the persona.

How can you easily spot a Cool Girl? She has a string of hot guy friends who hang around on the regular. They may or may not be sleeping together, no one is ever really sure, but the Guy Friend and the Cool Girl are definitely *bros.*

Ben was one of those guys.

Everything about him was warm. His eyes were dark and rimmed with thick, feathery black lashes. His smile made me feel like I'd just drunk from a deep mug of hot cocoa. Warm and sweet inside. He had the gift of making anyone feel like he'd known them forever, like they were the best of friends, like they were safe and cozy and warm when he was there.

He was in pre-law and casually mentioned that he hoped to work in women's rights and gender equality once he passed the bar. I almost got down on one knee and asked him to marry me. He was so handsome he nearly took my breath away. I relaxed quickly when I realized he was way out of my league so there was no point in feeling self-conscious or trying to impress him. Plus, like everyone else I assumed he was already sleeping with our local Cool Girl.

But it wasn't long before our Cool Girl friend dropped out of school and decided to move back to New York. Even though he and I still went to the same university, I didn't see Ben again for many months.

I was on a date with somebody else the next time I saw him. The guy was a twenty-five-year-old who lived in his parents' basement, thought Los Angeles was south of the equator, and had taken me to Tim Hortons for our first date. He also wore a backwards Maple Leafs baseball cap 100 percent of the time. I don't know what I was thinking: I'm a Habs fan.

"I really like Greek and Roman mythology," my date was telling me over his coffee. "Like Julius Caesar."

I gulped my drink to buy myself a few seconds. *What the hell am I supposed to say to that?* Cool Girls avoid correcting men as much as possible.

I got up under the pretence of fetching more milk for my tea and wondered how long I'd have to stay to avoid being rude.

"Nellwyn?"

It was him. Ben. The Impossibly Handsome Feminist.

He smiled at me like we were long-lost friends and pulled me in for a hug.

"How've you been?" he asked. "It's been ages."

"Good." I smiled. "Great."

"Is that your friend over there?" he asked, and pointed to my table.

"Uh, yeah. Definitely my *friend,*" I said.

"We should hang out and catch up sometime." He made it seem like we used to be the closest of friends.

"That would be great!" I said before walking back to my table a whole lot happier with my Friday night.

On our first date, I met Ben for a casual drink at a nearby pub. We sat in our booth until last call talking about all the dreams we had for our careers, the bands we loved, and our favourite foods. It was a flawless first date.

Only I wasn't completely sure if it *was* a date. It could easily have been nothing more than two friends catching up.

He didn't touch my hair or the hem of my shirt. He didn't touch me at all, in fact. He bought us drinks and I bought the second round. He walked me home, but he left me with only a hug.

Typical maybe-date.

Few young people ask each other out on actual dates anymore. Instead we ask each other to "hang out." I think people feel less likely to be rejected if their intentions aren't entirely clear. This way, you can always fall back on the delusion that you were only asking for company *as a friend.*

This contemporary trend results in a *lot* of maybe-dates.

Maybe-dates are tricky because you have to prepare for them as if they are real dates, but you also have to strike a balance so you don't look like you're trying too hard. You have to accept the fact that all the hard work you do shaving your legs and perfecting your smoky eye may be wasted.

Whenever I would find myself on a maybe-date, it was always very important to me that I find some way of clarifying the situation as soon as possible. This would prevent me from feeling like a fool and getting my hopes up for sex or a boyfriend or a date for next Friday. Actually *asking* if I was out on a date was absolutely out of the question. Doing that would ruin the unspoken agreement that we're both going to avoid rejection by simply "hanging out."

Hangout culture, as I'm going to call it, combined with the Myth of Men, is why I usually expected a kiss on a first date. I needed a foolproof way of knowing if you like me or *like*-like me. But because I believe in second chances and because I *really* believe in first-date jitters, I've almost always been willing to go on a second maybe-date if the first one was good. But if the guy didn't kiss me on the second date, I would assume he wasn't interested. After Tyler, after Jake, I vowed never again to chase after a guy who clearly didn't want me the way I wanted him.

For our second date, Ben and I upgraded from drinks to dinner. An upgrade like that indicates both parties can commit themselves to at least an hour with each other. It's a sign you've decided the other person isn't an axe murderer, a misogynist, or opposed to drinking before noon.

He took me to a little tapas place and I discovered the joys of dating a man who can appreciate good cuisine. I tried eating whole baby mackerel and choked down the bones because it seemed rude and unladylike to pick them out. When I got up halfway through the meal to use the washroom, I tried to walk away as if I knew he was watching me. I batted my eyelashes ever so briefly at the bartender. Not so much that Ben would think I wasn't interested in him, but just enough to make him the teensiest bit jealous if he needed to be.

He walked me home again and this time I thought I felt that elusive magnetic feeling. The feeling you get when you try and join two magnets with the same charge. The feeling that they're desperate to touch, but there's something insurmountable in the way. I usually left it to men to break the force field at times like that. I'd lean in, I'd play with my hair, but I would never make the first move.

We stood on the sidewalk in front of my house and made small talk. One more hug and this relationship was dead for sure. I remember seeing the look in his eyes change the moment he decided to go in for the kiss.

With the split-second warning, I was able to prepare. I reached up to put my hands around his neck and bent one knee slightly so I stood gracefully contrapposto like in a Renaissance painting. You know: the beautiful Venus, the epitome of love and sex and beauty gracefully rising from the sea. It also makes your hip jut out and your waist feel small and it makes tall girls like me a few inches shorter so you can feel like a girl in a fairy tale. Or so I thought.

After breaking up with Jake, it had been awhile since I'd kissed anyone sober, but he made me feel like I'd had three shots of Stolichnaya. It felt like we stood there together for hours, but I'm sure it was only a minute or two. I was more certain about this guy than I'd ever been about anyone before. The way he kissed me told me there would definitely be a third date.

The third date, according to arbitrary social constructions, is often the sex date.

If I thought our second date was an upgrade, the third certainly trumped it. The next week, I somehow managed to find an evening when all my many roommates were either in class, rehearsal, or at work. Since we'd have the entire house to ourselves, Ben offered to come over and cook dinner for me.

"What do you like to eat?" he asked.

"Everything," I said truthfully. "Except eel. And ketchup."

"So you like steak?"

"You just named my favourite food."

I'd just found a feminist lawyer-to-be who offered to cook me a steak. I'd woken up in dating heaven.

After dinner, we cozied up on the couch. Suddenly I was nervous. I'd had two glasses of wine, but it was rare that I contemplated having sex that sober. In fact, the only other time I'd been naked with a man without being drunk was with Jake, and we'd been dating for months by then.

I let Ben pull me in close. He stroked my arm gently and I looked up at him, but he didn't kiss me.

I got even more nervous.

I leaned against his chest as he brushed his fingers back and forth across the tiny little blond hairs on my forearm and I tried not to think about how heavy I must feel against him. The heat was on and I had a blanket at my feet, but somehow I felt cold. I felt goosebumps crawling along my skin as he breathed against my neck, but I was paralyzed. I stared out the window and listened as he spoke into the top of my head. We discussed the realities of legalizing prostitution in Canada and I wondered if he'd ever paid for sex. I wondered if I cared. I couldn't decide.

I don't remember exactly how we got to the bedroom, but I remember it took ages. Maybe I finally got up and led him there. Or maybe he finally leaned in on the sofa and kissed me, which seems more likely given my fear of rejection. But it seemed like the anticipation was worthwhile. By the time we got naked, I was thinking that, so far, this whole foreplay thing was going better than ever.

I tried to restrain the feeling that this was finally *the* moment. After so many mishaps and letdowns, I kept my expectations low. But this time, I would do one thing differently, something I would have found hard to forgive had the roles been reversed.

Unlike every guy I'd gone to bed with before, I lied by omission and didn't tell him I was a virgin. After so many rejections, I decided it was nobody's business but my own.

His shoulders were broad, his arms were strong, and I was more than ready.

We took off each other's clothes slowly and he hovered above me.

He didn't move.

I felt the blood rush into my head as my heart rate sped up a fraction. I was grateful for the dark as the heat rose in two bright patches on my cheeks. This wasn't embarrassment; it was shame. The feeling, not just that I had failed, but that I *was* a failure. I didn't know what it felt like to be desired, and more than ever, I knew I wasn't worthy of it. Other women made it look so easy, they had something that men wanted. I realized now that, whatever that was, I didn't have it. And without knowing what I was missing, I couldn't possibly hope to find it. The blood rushing to my head made the words stick in my throat when I spoke.

"What's wrong?" I asked.

"Nothing." He stared at my ribs.

"Do you want to stop?" I asked.

He had already stopped.

"Just tell me what's wrong," I said.

"No, it's embarrassing." He moved off me and lay face down with his head buried in my guest pillow.

"Well, it can't be worse than what I'm imagining," I said. "So you may as well tell me."

He hesitated. I let him sit in the silence. I knew it would come out eventually. Men look at me and they see a confessional.

"I think I have a problem ..."

"Okay." I tried to sound understanding.

"I think I watch too much pornography," he mumbled into my pillow, but there was no doubt about what he'd said.

I lay on my back in my bed, staring at the ceiling. I wasn't as shocked as many girls might have been since this was only the latest in my series of misfortunate adventures. I reached over the side of the bed and picked my underwear up off the floor. Victoria's Secret. Black cotton with a thick band of black lace trim. I grabbed the tank top crumpled next to it on the floor. Also black. Also trimmed with black lace. I sat on the edge of the bed to pull them on before lying back down to stare at the white ceiling. I tucked my forearm under my head and played with my hair.

Why does this always happen to me?

I felt stronger than I had been after the first few failed attempts. I think I even felt a little bit angry.

Ben finally turned his head to look at me.

"You okay?" he asked.

"Yeah," I said. "*I'm* fine."

"You're not upset?"

"No, I'm not." I felt a smile escape as I exhaled. "I'm just kicking myself."

"Why is that?" he asked carefully.

"Because I'd promised myself I wouldn't date anyone else who made me feel undesirable," I said bluntly.

I've always found it incredibly easy to be unabashedly honest with someone after they've seen me naked.

"I just got out of a relationship like that," I continued. "And I promised myself I would never do that again."

"Jeez," he said. "I'm sorry."

"Yeah well, it's not really your fault." I plumped up my pillow so I could lean against my headboard. "I'm just telling you I'm not going to go down that road again."

"I get that."

I wondered for a second if Ben was telling the truth about the porn, or if he was grasping for an escape route. But by then I knew what honest-to-god impotence looks like first-hand, and he was genuinely tortured by his confession.

He rolled over toward me and put his head on my chest. He snuggled against my neck and wrapped his arm around me. He rubbed his eyes and I caught him pushing back small little tears. Silently, his body asked me to comfort him and I knew he wasn't lying. I also knew there was no further discussion to be had.

I wanted to be alone. I wanted to Google erectile dysfunction and pornography. I wanted to wash off my makeup and put on my cozy pajamas. The men's boxers I'd bought two sizes too big and my oversized T-shirt with *Little Shop of Horrors* emblazoned on the chest, a memento from the first musical I ever sang in. I always felt better about myself, more confident, when I remembered I could sing a soprano solo in front of five hundred people.

But Ben hugged me tighter and burrowed his face between my breasts. I couldn't figure out what he was doing. Was he trying to rally himself or was he embarrassed and looking for comfort?

I let him nuzzle at me even though I kept picturing a baby rooting for milk. I touched his hair softly and looked into his eyes when he turned to face me. Dark chocolate-brown eyes that seemed to go on forever like deep dark holes into the very back of his brain. He didn't say anything else. He just turned his face back toward my chest and fell asleep.

I never did get to change into my *Little Shop of Horrors* T-shirt or wash my makeup off. I would have pimples on my chin for the rest of the week but at the time, that was the price to pay for having a man sleep in my bed. Being seen without makeup wouldn't become an option I'd feel good about for a few more years.

I slept uncomfortably. I wasn't used to being held all night. I remembered the way I'd carefully arranged my pillows and duvet all those years ago in high school so that I could pretend there was someone sleeping next to me. This wasn't at all what I'd imagined. Be careful what you wish for, they say. When God wants to punish us, he answers our prayers.

Ben left early in the morning before breakfast.

"Do you want to take some leftovers home?" I asked, simply because I didn't know what else to say.

"No, no," he said. "You keep them."

I would have given anything to trade leftover steak for a boyfriend.

To write that I was disappointed wouldn't quite explain the feeling I had that morning. I'd run out of disappointment by then. It was more disbelief that I had failed yet again, mixed with the strange feeling that perhaps this was my destiny. Maybe I was to move through life like some mystical virgin who prompts men to face their true selves. Or maybe I was just pathetic.

I never saw Ben after that morning. The following September, he moved away for law school. When an intelligent news article about Canadian politics popped up on my Facebook feed it was often shared by him, but seeing his name above the headline was the closest I ever got to him again.

* * * * *

Years later, at home in Toronto on a chilly, late September evening, I was lying in bed with a big glass of cheap California Cab and watching sex-positive feminist comedian Chelsea Handler host her new Netflix talk show.

I was paying more attention to the succulents on my Instagram feed and was only half-listening to the banter, until I heard Handler introduce a pair of guests.

I slammed my wine down on my nightstand and threw my phone to the other side of the bed. I sat up and piled all my pillows behind my back so I could sit comfortably at attention.

There they were, right in front of me on my computer screen.

The men I'd been looking for.

Noah B.E. Church and Gabe Deem sat comfortably on Chelsea's interview couch and talked openly about their negative experiences with internet porn. These two trendily dressed twenty-somethings were no Bible-clutching sex-negative moralistic preachers. They were two millennial guys who, in their own words, were "told that porn would be sex-positive and it ended up being completely sex-negative."[2]

I understood that statement immediately. I had also grown up thinking pornography was a sex-positive way to explore your sexuality. I thought that the people who placed the blue pamphlets around my town cautioning against the dangers of pornography and sex addiction were sex-negative religious folk who wanted to keep us held back in a former era of repression and sexual shame.

I listened to people like Dan Savage who insisted "all men watch porn" and that it was time women got on board with this harmless form of sexual fantasy.[3]

I assumed my boyfriend, if I ever really had one, would watch porn, and I was okay with that.

When I was in my third year of university and casually mentioned to my roommates that I'd never seen pornography, they were shocked. They hauled me upstairs to show me what I was missing and chose a clip of two men having sex next to an indoor swimming pool for my porn initiation. It was called *Beautiful Sons of the Ancient World*, and I think the swimming pool was supposed to replicate an ancient Roman bathhouse or something.

I think the fact that I hadn't seen pornography until I was twenty was so shocking to my friends because we are the first generation to grow up with such easy access to it, thanks to the internet. We don't remember the days of stealing your dad's *Playboy*s to look at a handful of nudie shots. A friend of mine born in 1980 had a completely different teenage experience with pornography than those of us born in the nineties.

"I remember crowding around the computer with my buddy when we were, like, fifteen to watch one picture of Pamela Anderson download inch by inch," he told me. "It took forever to see one picture. Nowadays everything is oversaturated. There's just too much porn."

Church and Deem seemed to agree with that statement on Chelsea Handler's talk show. Both men have suffered from pornography addiction and porn-induced erectile dysfunction (PIED), and are now working to raise awareness and help other people recover from similar problems. Church is the author of *Wack: Addicted to Internet Porn* and Deem runs an online porn recovery community at RebootNation.org.

"When I was twelve," Deem said, "my family got high-speed internet and then I started watching internet porn. I would ride my bike home from school and watch porn for a couple hours before my parents got home. And it was a normal part of teen culture.... Our generation is the first generation that grew up with unlimited access to internet porn. We're not talking magazines or cave drawings. We're talking where you can have multiple videos open at the same time ... while you jack off to one video, you can search for other videos at the same time. That's something that no one's been able to do in human history before."

Eager to learn more, I visited Noah B.E. Church's website to get my hands on a copy of his book. Sitting in a very fancy Parisian-style café with my laptop on a huge solid white marble tabletop, I was thrilled to discover that *Wack: Addicted to Internet Porn* was available as a free PDF download. All I had to do to download my free copy instantly was sign up for Noah Church's mailing list. I took a sip of my fancy tea out of my big white mug and signed up for regular updates on recovering from porn addiction while a mother sitting next to me bounced her baby on her lap and ate little bites of croissant.

Within minutes, the book arrived in my inbox. Despite all the porn out there, I do really love the internet.

Drawing on a study done by addiction specialist Dr. Jennifer P. Schneider, Church writes, "If you are a porn-watching man (especially a young man) in generally good health who has lost interest in real sex or has difficulty 'getting it up' or keeping it up with a partner, porn use is probably the cause."

We're all used to hearing stories from men who complain that their spouse or partner isn't sexually adventurous enough or attractive enough anymore, but, as Church says, "It is near impossible for any lone woman to compete with the dopamine rush that a porn addict gets when using."[4]

Okay. So what has led the author to his conclusions, aside from his own personal experience? And what does dopamine have to do with it all? As someone who grew up thinking that porn/sex addiction is a myth created by right-wing religious zealots, I went looking for the science behind this new phenomenon.

I dove into the world of neuroplasticity and learned the catch-phrase: "neurons that fire together wire together." This means that when two neurons in the brain fire together repeatedly, they connect to each other and form pathways in the brain called brain maps. According to relatively new science that has proved the plasticity of the brain, this type of long-term neuroplastic change is at the root of all addictions.

For example, when a person views pornography, a neurological connection is created between the images on screen and the pleasure centres of the brain. This connection is reinforced by the dopamine released in the brain during orgasm because dopamine is the brain's reward chemical.

In plain English, porn addicts have developed new maps in their brains by repeatedly associating pornographic content with sexual pleasure and release. And "when we develop a map area, we long to keep it activated."[5]

Cue addiction.

Like addiction to drugs and alcohol, serious pornography addictions can affect one's social life, sleep habits, work ethic, and interest in other non-porn-related activities. Also, similar to other types of addicts, porn addicts quickly become desensitized to the images they see and require higher and higher levels of stimulation to get the same results. Desensitization to the pleasure-causing substance, whether it be alcohol, drugs, or porn, is one of the hallmarks of addiction. This is one reason why we see more and more hardcore, violent, and degrading pornography going mainstream. With so much of the violence in pornography directed toward women, combined with ubiquitous media representations of women as perpetually sexually available, I can begin to understand how the term "incel" and its violent connotations came to be.

After a student in Santa Barbara shot and killed six women in 2014, a video surfaced in which the killer expressed his desire to murder women who had rejected him sexually. This incident is often cited as the first crime perpetrated by an "incel" or "involuntary celibate." "Incels" are self-identifying men who are unable to find a romantic or sexual partner and typically find community in online subcultures. After the Santa Barbara shooting, a series of other incidents of violent public misogyny have been attributed to the rise of this subculture. As we discussed this strange phenomenon, my thirty-something male friend shook his head.

"Too much porn," he said again. "And too much *Grand Theft Auto*. Kids now feel entitled to sex from women because that's all they see online. Submissive porn stars. And they think they deserve that from real women."

Speaking about a notorious "cheat mode" in *Grand Theft Auto V* that made headlines the same year as the Santa Barbara tragedy, he added, "I mean, there's actually a video game where it's part of the game to rape women. And nine-year-old kids are playing this. It's disgusting." While it would be reductive and irresponsible to make too many knee-jerk leaps and connections between misogynistic violence, pornography, and video games, the omnipresence of sexualized and violent media should be a concern for anyone living in a culture where a movement like "incel" has recently been born.

If we turn back to the brain, we can begin to understand some of the connections that may be at play. Many patients in treatment for porn addiction report seeking out hardcore images and videos that they themselves find degrading or disgusting, but their desensitized brain maps make them seek it out, regardless.

Desensitization or functional tolerance is easy to understand even without an education in neuroplasticity. I used to be able to get drunk off a couple ounces of vodka. Now I need three martinis before wanting to dance on a tabletop.

After my introductory viewing of *Beautiful Sons of the Ancient World*, I've watched pornography only a handful of times, but it didn't take long for me to notice a desensitization in myself. It probably took ten or fifteen minutes of watching "vanilla" porn clips before I got bored and clicked the "hardcore" tab in the website menu.

Working in the restaurant industry throughout my twenties, it wasn't long before I started craving a drink every night at 10:00 p.m.

The brain can change very quickly.

It's easy to understand why I wasn't exciting enough for Ben.

I'm a real person.

So what about all the sex-positive scholars and advice columnists out there who maintain that pornography is healthy and normal?

Of course, there is also a wide range of ethical and empowering pornography available, and there are plenty of people who enjoy pornography without it having any negative impact on their lives or relationships. Just like how there are plenty of casual drinkers, recreational drug users, and occasional gamblers who don't fall into addiction or destructive behaviours. I know these people. I'm friends with them. I drink and do recreational drugs with them. And sometimes I talk about porn with them.

When I started interviewing people and talking to the outside world about this book, I noticed a pattern emerging where pornography was concerned. Many twenty-something girls I spoke with knew someone or had been sexual with someone whose porn habits were negatively impacting their life. When I spoke with guys, no one confessed to having PIED themselves, but every single one had a friend or a friend-of-a-friend who did. After a lot of requests, I finally managed to find one of these friends-of-friends who agreed to be interviewed, but at the last minute he jumped on a plane to Melbourne and stopped returning my emails. Fair enough.

In-person confessions of porn addiction, particularly when faced with the prospect of your words appearing in print, are rare. However, in more anonymous circles, the truth comes out in waves. There is an entire sub-forum on the website reddit, which is a collection of forums on all subjects, devoted entirely to the "NoFap" movement. NoFap is internet shorthand for quitting porn and masturbation. This forum has more than 426,000 subscribers, and when I logged on at 1:30 p.m. on a Monday afternoon, there were 1,700 active users.* Scrolling through the first page of discussions, the forum reminded me of a virtual meeting of Alcoholics Anonymous.

Some people share their success stories with post titles like "Day 100!!," "I did it," and "2 Years PMO free." (PMO is shorthand for porn, masturbation, orgasm.) Others seek out the forum for advice, support, and accountability with posts like "Relapsed after 60 days" and "If I make it to 30 days, I'll buy myself an iPad."[6] The NoFap forum even makes it possible for users to put little badges next to their usernames that indicate how many days they've gone without PMO. It's the internet equivalent of an alcoholic's sobriety chip. The similarities between different types of addiction continue to get even stronger.

Some forum topics discussed how quitting porn changed a man's attitude toward women. A user with a ten-day badge wrote that he'd just visited Reddit's fetish sub-forum and continued, "It

* As I rewrote and edited this book, Reddit's NoFap forum continued to grow with each revision of the manuscript. It grew from just over 377,000 subscribers in November 2018 to 424,000 subscribers by April 9, 2019. When I checked again only six days later, it had already jumped up to over 426,000.

is fucking disgusting to see where I came from and where I am now. I couldn't be more proud to know I don't dwell with those psychos anymore."[7] After twenty-four days of NoFap, another man posted:

> Before I began my NoFap journey, I objectified the hell out of women. Yes, I am ashamed to admit that. All I could think about was what I would like to do with her.... One of the things that my reboot has done for me, now I look at a woman, and it doesn't matter their shape, size or whatever, I think to myself that this is a person who has feelings, needs and wants and is a human being. This person could be going through shit that I don't even know and they deserve all the respect that I can give them.[8]

As damaging as I think certain types of porn can be in terms of contributing to increases in sexual violence, objectification, and misogyny, I do think it's equally dangerous to categorize all fetishists and porn users as sexual psychopaths. I agree with the sex-positive idea that people shouldn't be ashamed of their kinks and that sexual experimentation can be healthy and fun. We can't ignore the possibility that ethically made pornography might be a boon to healthier and more inclusive understandings of human sexuality. However, ethical and inclusive pornographies have not yet achieved the pervasiveness and accessibility of mainstream erotica, which is too often exactly the opposite.

These complexities are part of why talking about porn can quickly get you into hot water. As we begin to become more aware of the unprecedented ubiquity of porn and its consequences (positive and negative), there is a lot of disagreement about what this all means.

While studies are emerging on the risks of porn/sex addiction, PIED, and more, there are other groups of academics and researchers who question or deny the existence of these conditions. Whatever your opinion on the impacts of pornography, you can likely find a study to support your argument — such is the conflicting nature of the research at this stage.

While it's easy to summarize opposing arguments as the views of two separate camps, there is also a lot of room for shifting and nuance in our understandings as we all begin to learn more about the potential impacts of this unprecedented access and exposure to porn.

I think it's impossible to settle on a definitive opinion on pornography; studies are still emerging and often conflicting, and there is too wide a range of pornography types and genres. Barely anyone I know has heard the official term "porn-induced erectile dysfunction," but it seems like everyone has a negative porn-related anecdote to share ... at least when the anecdote involves a friend-of-a-friend.

When I found myself craving a glass of wine every night at 10:00 p.m., I drank water instead. I'd been educated about the risks of alcoholism, functional tolerance, and its warning signs, so I took care of myself. We need to educate people about the risks of pornography in the same way, without demonizing or shaming healthy sexual exploration. Porn is not inherently sex-positive or sex-negative, just like alcohol is not inherently good or evil.

But it's time for the sex-positive movement to stop espousing its virtues as a purely harmless and healthy form of sexual expression. Regardless of where you fall on the question of pornography, we need to start having more and better conversations about *both* the potential risks and benefits of porn to our sexual and mental health.

For men, the symptoms of PIED go beyond erectile dysfunction itself and lead to other relationship-killing feelings of shame, anxiety, depression, isolation, and low self-esteem. When faced with a partner who is unknowingly suffering from PIED, women (and men) feel many of the same feelings, often blaming themselves and descending into similar emotional chasms.

Years ago, when Ben fell asleep with his head on my chest, I trusted the sex-positive movement. Like many women, I hadn't done any of this research and I didn't understand what I was facing, so I put the blame on myself. After Ben left in the morning, I put on my boxer shorts and oversized T-shirt and crawled back into bed. Would I ever be good enough for someone to want me?

I was really starting to doubt it.

Failing, yet again, to lose my virginity was about more than simply being unable to live up to pornography's unrealistic standards. I was hit deeply by the realization that I was in way over my head. Not only did I not know how to deal with pornography addiction, I realized that I didn't know how to deal with *anything* to do with sex. At least not any of the real things. Sure, I had all my accumulated knowledge from books and magazines and podcasts and gossip, but I had not acquired one single piece of knowledge that I could actually *use*.

Every time I got together with a new guy, I got hit with a new challenge. Each boy I dated gave me something new to worry about, something I was afraid would come up again that I still wouldn't know how to handle. Ben gave me the fear that every time I failed to live up to a man's fantasies, I would have to talk myself out of a brand-new psychological shame spiral to drag my self-esteem back up where it belongs.

I felt exhausted at the sheer thought of dating. Beyond all else, it seemed impossibly unfair. With everything I'd learned, experienced, and put up with so far, here was yet *another* trial that no one, including me, had thought to prepare for.

But this is how I learned to be more cautious in my relationship with the sex-positive movement and to apply more critical thinking to its tenets. After all, no movement can account for all the complexities of human experience.

Our sexual struggles and imperfections have far more power over us than they should. I wanted to believe that I could separate my sexual failures from my sense of self, but as I lay in bed that morning after Ben left, it seemed completely impossible.

CHAPTER 13

A S UPSET AS I WAS over the Ben Incident, it wasn't long before I met someone who gave me a sudden and surprising new sense of hope. Have you ever met someone and known that it was only a matter of time before you hook up? I met Dave on a boring night in when my roommates and I decided to play Truth or Dare. His friend was going out with one of the girls in our house and the two guys decided to stop by on their way home from the pub.

Dave was very good-looking in an obviously athletic kind of way. He walked with a masculine confidence that most of the boys in theatre school didn't have. He was broad-shouldered and tall, he ran marathons and played sports. I bet he was a gladiator in a past life. I could see him walking in to face a lion with his head held high, strong and tough. Bronze breastplate. Sword held aloft. Dusty, sweaty, aggressive.

I was wearing pink leopard print from head to toe when we met. A Truth or Dare casualty.

I sprawled on the floor while he held his head in his hands and complained about his recent ex-girlfriend.

Perfect.

It was only a matter of time.

I can't explain it, but there was that *thing* between us, that electric *thing*. The *thing* made it seem like hooking up was the only natural progression for our relationship.

I saw him again at a charity dodgeball match we'd all signed up for. He was on the Athletic-Engineering-Student Team and I was on the Silly-Artsy-Girls-Who-Like-To-Wear-Leopard-Print Team.

I'd never cared about a sport so much in my life. I raced around the court, determined to show off and determined to win. I watched Dave out of the corner of my eye. There's something that happens when you like someone. An awareness so heightened that it keeps them at the front of your brain regardless of where you are or how many times you've been hit in the head with a dodgeball. It's as if they glow, so you can always see them, always feel them, no matter where they are. That light pulls your focus and it's so very hard to look away. The question, the desperate all-consuming question, becomes whether or not you're glowing, too. Has he not looked at me because he, too, is blinded by the light? Or is he just trying to win a game of dodgeball?

"You two should get together," his friend said to me a few days later. "He's basically over his ex by now. And he's going through a really hard time. He could use someone like you."

"What do you mean?" I asked.

"His mother's not very well, she's in and out of the hospital all the time. Comas. Cancer."

I was a little surprised Dave had never mentioned this, but then I remembered that he wasn't like most of the guys I knew. Being a theatre major means that you regularly participate in emotional-connection exercises and curriculum-mandated diary-writing, so I was used to seeing my guy friends open up and get vulnerable. At the same time, outside of the classroom, many of them went above and beyond to shore up a stereotypical masculine identity that had no place in theatre school. It was like they had to make up for the fact that they were so in touch with their feelings by working out a lot and giving their houses really masculine-sounding names like Bro Base and Das Haus (yes, those are real house names from my past).

I wasn't really sure what to make of a guy like Dave. He wasn't particularly emotional, and he also didn't appear to be working overtime to show off his masculinity. He seemed so uncomplicated compared to us theatre students who were always analyzing and deconstructing our feelings as part of our homework. I understood that he might want to keep his mom's health issues private, and decided not to bring it up unless he mentioned it first.

Spring was arriving and we decided to throw another one of our famous house parties. Setting up to throw a house party was like preparing to host a stampede of wild animals in our living room. Everything breakable was hidden away in the kitchen cabinets and stacks of plastic cups were lined along the counter so no one would go searching through the cupboards for a real glass. We hauled the largest cardboard box we could find on campus all the way home to serve as our Dumpster and placed it conspicuously next to the kitchen counter. Our little box on top of the fridge where we kept our emergency condoms and a couple of half-smoked joints was hidden from anyone desperate enough to steal even that tiny bit of weed. I'd been to parties where the hosts had covered their floors in cardboard to catch any spills, but our carpets were already ruined by a few too many vomit stains for us to bother going to that much trouble.

My bedroom was spotless and my sheets were clean. You never knew who would show up at our parties. *Everyone* was invited after all.

A year later, I became friends with a former classmate who never came to any of our parties.

"I wasn't invited," he said.

"It's a *party*," was my response. "*Everyone* was invited."

"Well, not everyone felt like they could go."

This was the first time I realized that our way of living — of socializing, of partying — was not necessarily normal. It always seemed like everyone in college partied hard and slept around and had friends who threw up on their carpet, but maybe not. I always thought our group seemed hospitable and friendly and fun, but it turns out not everyone saw us that way.

Partying the way we did — binge-drinking, hooking up, smoking weed, and sampling hard drugs — was part of how we constructed our identities as cool, popular, desirable, savvy, liberated feminists. And all those activities were so closely linked it was almost impossible to separate them from one another. You couldn't party without drinking, you couldn't have casual sex without partying *and* drinking, and the drugs were there to prove we weren't afraid. We thought we were just the right kind of bad.

We were liberated, and we proved it to the world twice a week, every week, on Friday and Saturday nights.

Dave came in, looking handsome as ever, at just the right time. The party was in full swing, but I hadn't drunk enough yet to have started making a fool of myself.

On the surface, this party was just like all the others. I drank vodka and grapefruit juice. I wore tight jeans and a low-cut top. The music was loud. The drugs of choice were cocaine for the pros and MDMA for those just beginning to dabble in the hard stuff. Hallucinogens were a bad idea for a crowd of people with such overactive imaginations. But this party was different. This was the last college party we would throw. Graduation was less than a month away. The entire night had a Last Supper kind of feeling.

If there was anything you wanted to say, anything (or any*one*) you wanted to do, this was your chance.

I sat on the sofa with my legs crossed and held my drink in a real glass (one of the many benefits of being a host). Sitting down at a party or backstage in a green room shows you're in control. People have to come to you. You're too cool to care about mingling and making connections and throwing yourself at people. You're content. Confident. Less likely to do something stupid.

The engineering boys stood out from the crowd. They had nothing to prove. Their jeans fit a little looser, their sneakers were a little more expensive. Dave walked over to the vintage Victorian-style couch I'd perched myself on and stood in front of me.

"Do you want to go outside?" he asked.

It was freezing cold and there was nowhere interesting to go in our pre-fab suburb.

"Sure." I grabbed my coat and made my way to the kitchen where half my roommates were doing shots.

"Where are you guys going?"

"Outside."

"Why?"

I shrugged and put on my boots while the girls stared at me, half-surprised, half-knowing what would happen next.

Our backyard was far from private, the big kitchen windows looked directly out onto the tiny postage stamp of grass we called ours, and there were about twenty drunk soon-to-be graduates staring out at us. Dave took my hand and led me into the alley between the neighbour's garage and ours. This wasn't the first time I'd found myself wedged between a man and an alley wall, but this time it felt even more intimate, as if that night was darker than others and we were really alone in the world. I couldn't hear the music coming from the house anymore. There didn't seem to be any stars. The little groups of students who wound their way from house to house with six-packs of beer and pockets full of weed must have all settled into their parties by now. No headlights, no raccoons, nothing.

He pulled me close against him and kissed me.

"I've wanted to do that forever," he said.

I knew it.

I was triumphant.

"Me too," I said.

Triumphant people can afford to be generous, plus it was true.

"Ever since that dodgeball game," he said. "My god."

Then why didn't you do anything until now?

"Mm-hmm."

My coat was open and I was freezing cold, but his hands were unbuttoning my pants and I didn't want to go inside. I worried someone would come around the corner and see him with his hands inside my jeans, but it was so dark and I'd waited so long.

I tried not to shiver as my shirt slid up and exposed more of my stomach. I bit my lips to keep my teeth from chattering and pulled my hands into the arms of my coat sleeves.

"Let's go upstairs," I finally suggested.

The party was dark, but all the eyes were like searchlights following us through the kitchen and upstairs. We stumbled into my bedroom and I closed the door behind us. A little light trickled in through its frosted glass panels and I took off my coat. We could hear the party going on all around us as he lay back on the bed.

I took off my shirt so we wouldn't have to start talking.

By now I was feeling pretty confident that I knew my way around some decent foreplay. It wasn't long before we were both undressed and perfectly poised to kick things off. His shadow above me was just a darker shape against my black ceiling.

I waited for something to happen.

This feeling was familiar.

Or should I say, this lack of feeling was familiar.

I looked into his eyes for the first time and saw from the moonlight in the window that they were glistening with tears.

"What's wrong?"

"I'm sorry," he said. "I can't."

"It's fine. Are you okay?"

He rolled off me and into the crook of my arm. I held him like a child and stroked his hair softly.

"It's my mom," he said. "She's so sick. She's in the hospital —"

"It's okay," I whispered.

We lay together like that for such a long time. Me holding him while he cried softly. I didn't let go and he didn't pull away. I wondered what it was about me that causes people to open up so fully. Is it because I have big eyes? Is it because I look like a Jane Austen character? Or is it because I bake pies and let them cool on windowsills?

In the soft moonlight, I could see the tears clinging to the corners of his eyes. I stroked my fingers through his hair as gently as I could because that's what I would have wanted someone to do for me. I forgot that we were naked. I forgot how little we knew each other.

I wanted to feel angry, but it was a distant anger. I was angry that I was the one who always seemed to have to deal with the big feelings of the boys I went to bed with. Why did the other girls get to have all the fun? Why did I always have to be the one taking care of everybody else? I did it and I did it graciously because that's the right thing to do when someone is crying naked in your arms, but again I asked myself, *What is it about* me? *And why the hell did nobody tell me this might happen?* I wasn't at all angry at Dave, if anything I was sad for him. But I was angry at my friends, at my mother, at fucking *Cosmopolitan*, and everyone else who had led me to believe that it was easy to just *relax and have fun.* Maybe it is for some people. But it sure wasn't easy for me, and it wasn't easy for the boys, either.

Dave stopped crying and we lay together until I felt all the alcohol I'd drunk start to sink in.

"I'm just going to go to the washroom," I said. "I'll be right back. Do you want to stay here or do you want to go back to the party?"

"No, let's go back to the party."

I pulled a sweater on over my jeans. I wasn't in the mood to get back into my sexy outfit.

"Okay, I'll meet you there."

I thought he might want a few minutes alone.

But I never saw him again.

• • ● • •

So much has been written about men and their tears that I hesitate to reiterate it here. After thousands of years of "be a man" and "tears are for pussies," the real-men-show-emotion movement has made serious strides. Nowadays, men are encouraged to show emotion and even to cry — but only under a very specific set of circumstances: weddings, funerals, breakups, births, the death of a sports hero or rock legend are all acceptable tear-shedding moments. Before, during, or after sex are not. But I wouldn't necessarily chalk that up to sexism or expectations of masculinity. I would argue that it's rarely socially acceptable to cry during sex no matter what your gender may be. Although women do tend to get a little more leeway any time emotions are concerned.

Since there are already pages and pages of gender theory written on the relationship between men and their tears, I'm going to move on to the Triangle of Doom that I believe is responsible for Dave ghosting me.

The Triangle of Doom exists when you connect the dots between sex, oppressive gender norms, and emotional intimacy.

Social and cultural changes over the last several decades have divorced sex from its marriage to emotional intimacy. The assumption that the two will always go together, particularly for women, no longer exists.

It's arguable that, for men, sex and emotional intimacy have always been separable and the changes in recent decades have simply been to put women on an even playing field by eliminating that oppressive double standard. A big part of the sexual liberation movement has been about proving that women can have casual, emotion-free sex "like men."

And, *yes*, we can.

I am from a generation that believes emotional intimacy often develops *after* you sleep with someone. Weeks or months after, and sometimes never. Sex is another way to find out if you're compatible enough with a person to take the risk of falling in love, of getting attached, of being emotionally intimate. Whether or not this has always been the case for men, and women are just recently exerting the same freedom, is unclear to me at this point but, regardless, the ties between sex and love have been severed for everyone. Often, those ties are only reunited when, at some point *after* a couple has been sleeping together for a while, one of them brings up the word "exclusive" or the phrase "where is this going?" That rejoining of the ties happens at different points in different relationships, but I think most people would agree that it's usually somewhere between one and six months.

The point I'm trying to make is that many people of my generation don't think of sex as a de facto emotionally intimate experience. One day in our fourth year of university, after one of my friends had been dating her boyfriend for close to a year, she came up with the three categories of sex as we had experienced it. (Well, not as *I*, personally, had experienced yet, but you know what I mean.)

We were lounging in our living room on a Sunday afternoon, wearing different combinations of sweatpants and hoodies embroidered with our school name and major. Cups of tea in varying states of freshness were scattered around the room and the kettle was boiling in the kitchen. One girl let her legs drape over the armchair as she scrolled through internet forums on her pink laptop. Another sat cross-legged on the floor, painting her nails. A third was surrounded by books on the sofa, reading the best bits aloud whenever she came across something that spoke to our artistic souls. I can picture them perfectly, but I'm not sure what I was doing. I was likely curled up in a ball on the futon with a book or a laptop of my own. Or perhaps I was stretching on the floor or painting my nails, too. We were distracted by a knock on the door. Our friend Amy was on the back stoop, having stopped by after walking her boyfriend Jeff to the bus stop at the end of our street. She plopped herself down on the end of the sofa, tucked her legs underneath her body, and sighed.

"I've realized something," she said. "There are three kinds of sex."

She sounded like she'd been waiting to tell us this all morning.

"There's having sex. Which is just the routine, basic, like, physical act of having sex. You know, sex that's just … mechanical."

Two of the girls started to nod.

"And then there's fucking, which is like 'Ohmygod, I want to make you come so hard,' and it's super hot and intense …"

"Yeah."

"And then there's making love. You know, when you feel that connection with someone and you're actually *making love.*"

She paused for effect.

"Well, last night, for the first time, I feel like Jeff and I made love."

"Wow, that's so amazing!"

"Good for you!"

"I'm so happy for you!"

Amy beamed. It only took a year or so for sex and intimacy to come together in her relationship.

Needless to say, when I started hooking up with guys, I didn't expect emotions to come into play since they were supposed to develop later. The problem is that despite everything the sexual revolution has done to give women the rightful freedom to have casual, emotion-free sex, I'm not sure it's really as easy or as simple as we've been led to believe.

No one prepared me for the watershed moment. No one warned me that sex has the power to unleash some of our most repressed thoughts and fears regardless of whether or not those feelings have anything to do with the sex itself.

Half of the Triangle of Doom is covered by sex and intimacy, but what about sex and gender norms?

Pervasive, but narrow and repressive, ideas about gender present unrealistic and often sexist ideals that can shape our behaviours at the expense of our needs. Sex is an experience where, due to its nature, we are often the most vulnerable to damaging expectations of what masculinity and femininity "should" look like.

In an anonymous online forum, a group of men were asked the following question: "What is your main method of feeling manly? (Gym, sports, drinking with friends, etc.)"

Here are two of my favourite answers:

"I feel the most manly when I'm fucking my wife."

"I guess working out and banging my girlfriend?"[1]

For many people, having sex means being a *man*. And, to be honest, how couldn't it?

From a purely biological perspective, sex demands a rush of testosterone, the most masculine of hormones. And then all a guy has to do is look down and he'll see his dick double in size. What could possibly make you feel more manly? I get it, I really do.

So, yes, sex may be thought of as among the most masculine of acts, but the problem that creates the Triangle of Doom is that it is also among the most intimate, the most emotional. And thanks to outdated gender norms, many men still struggle to reconcile those two realities. This is particularly challenging in a culture where expectations of masculinity make it difficult for men to express their emotions or tap into their vulnerability in a conscious way. Without a healthy emotional outlet, it becomes more likely that the vulnerability of sex will unlock bigger issues.

But wait? Didn't I just say we'd succeeded in creating a norm of emotionally detached sex among both men and women?

Well, we think we have.

But we've made a Crucial Mistake.

We have convinced ourselves that we are in control of all our emotions pre-, during, and post-coitus.

I've often thought that having feelings during a hookup meant I was too emotional.

A delusional romantic.

A girl who'd watched too many Disney movies.

A bad feminist.

Having feelings too early in a sexual relationship meant your heart lived in your vagina. And *that* means you aren't really in control of the situation. Your heart belongs to whatever guy happens to be poking around in there at the time. The idea that sex, for women, inherently comes with feelings, with attachment, with love is a narrative that has kept women on an unequal sexual playing field for centuries. It's what we've told our daughters to convince them to stay home on Friday nights knitting tea cozies. To be a feminist today means that you can (and should) have sex like a man.

That's where we start getting to our Crucial Mistake.

Why do men and their stereotypes have to be the barometer for female sexual empowerment?

I believe we *can* have sex without emotion, and I believe it because I've seen it. I've done it. But the Crucial Mistake is that we can never *guarantee* which of our encounters will be feelings-free. And that goes for *both* men and women.

Feelings are like termites. You never know when those creepy motherfuckers are going to sneak into your carefully constructed casual-sex townhouse and turn the whole thing to sawdust.

That being said, I think we're ready and willing to accept the occasional termite-of-feelings among women more so than among men.

Even though it's become acceptable for men to express emotion and tears, it's still framed within the idea that, in doing so, men are getting in touch with their feminine side. Expressing emotion has not become associated with masculinity. It is merely an aspect of femininity that men are encouraged to embrace under the guise of being a more well-rounded human being.

I kept investigating to find out if any other girls had encountered an unexpected rush of male emotion (i.e., tears) that cut a sexual encounter unfortunately short. In a forum titled "Ask Men," a group of men were asked point blank: "Have you ever cried after sex?"

My favourite answers:

"Only from my penis."

"Maybe a tear from a painful leg cramp."

"I've cried a few weeks after having sex while chopping onions."

"Maybe if she bites my dick off."

To be fair, some men confessed to crying during or after sex in long-term relationships, usually when they were about to be separated from their partner for a long period of time. Like moving away for graduate school or being shipped overseas with the military.

One of the first questions I wanted to ask when I starting interviewing men was about this connection between sex and emotional intimacy. With very little prompting on my part, both of my first two interviewees launched into stories of their own.

Hector, a former co-worker of mine, told me about a friends-with-benefits relationship he had while on an exchange trip in Spain. The girl had a serious boyfriend back home, so her agreement with Hector was that their relationship be completely free of emotional strings.

"How was that?" I asked.

"Disaster," Hector said. "Because I ended up falling in love with her."

"Oh god. How soon?"

"Almost immediately, actually."

I wondered if he'd secretly been in love with her all along, perhaps even since the day they'd met.

"In retrospect," he continued, "everything was there, you know? I found her physically attractive, I enjoyed her company, I enjoyed talking to her. She had everything."

"It's easy to fall in love with your friends," I said. I should know, it's one of my worst habits.

"Yeah, but until I actually slept with her … I don't know, I thought I'd be able to just continue having that friendship but you know … I knew she had a boyfriend in Toronto and was going to go back to that when the whole study-abroad program was finished, but I didn't want it to end, so things got complicated."

I nodded sympathetically to show that I understood unrequited love, that this interview wasn't just some social experiment. And then I asked, "Would you do friends-with-benefits again?"

Without hesitation, Hector abandoned his usual soft-spoken tone and replied, "No."

My Irish friend Oliver had a similar story about a girl he'd hooked up with after a party in his early twenties.

"After that I really wanted to be with her."

One night not long after, Oliver was hanging out on his friend Mike's balcony, drinking beers and telling him all about this girl.

"Listen, do you like her?" Mike asked.

"Yes," Oliver said.

"Do you really like her?"

"Yes."

"Then what are you doing on this balcony?"

That was all it took. Oliver got in his car.

"I called her up and told her how much I really wanted to be with her, and that is was so necessary and blah blah blah. I think I said some horrible clichés. I drove round to her house and had to jump down the back fence so I wouldn't wake her parents. I went around the back and knocked on her bedroom window. I climbed through … and then we got together after that."

Always one to spoil a perfect movie moment, and comfortable that Oliver wouldn't be offended, I had to ask, "I'm assuming you didn't just want to be with her after the sex because she was really good in bed?"

Oliver laughed. "No, it was something else.… We knew we were very close, we knew we were attracted to each other.… So I think what ended up happening was that by having sex, and solidifying that emotional and physical connection, it made me feel like it should be a thing."

"So having sex with her allowed you to feel the full extent of your feelings?"

"Yeah."

Although Hector and Oliver both fell head over heels in relationships that they'd expected would stay casual, I was having a hard time finding another interview subject similar to Dave, who found himself, not in love, but in pain. Despite the hyperconnectivity of the internet age, Dave and I were not friends on any social media platform and I don't remember his last name. Unable to track him down, I combed through a lot more online forums and personal essays on women's lifestyle websites.

I could not find a single record of any story remotely similar to what I'd experienced with Dave.

But here's what I do know.

Sex isn't always the flippant, casual act of fun-and-games-and-orgasms that we'd like it to be. Sometimes it has the power to unlock something we've been repressing or ignoring. Something wonderful, like love. Something painful, tragic, or vulnerable. Something that may have nothing to do with the sex or the relationship itself. And what we *don't* know is when those emotions and feelings and fears are going to stay safely in the darkest corners of our minds and when they're going to burst forward and ruin an otherwise excellent Friday night.

I will never tell you to stay home knitting tea cozies to avoid getting your heart broken or to reduce the risk of getting your snot and tears all over a stranger's naked shoulder. Go out, get laid, cry, and then cry harder. But please remember: being a feminist shouldn't mean having sex "like a man," and it's high time that men start to rethink what that means as well. All the empowerment in the world won't change the truth: sex is designed to make you *feel*, and some feelings simply can't be ignored.

The men in my life have had a habit of imprinting on me. I hear their deepest confessions, their darkest secrets, and they weave into my arms so I can stroke their hair and tell them everything will be all right before they fall asleep.

Too often I get mistaken for a delicate storybook character who reminds men of the virgin woman they would have courted chastely and married in some country church if they'd been born two hundred years earlier. My eyes are too big, my smile is too wide, my face is too soft. For some reason, I invoke confessions. Or I remind men of their mothers.

I suppose the truth is that for all my drinking and flirting and partying, I was still that little girl from the country who liked to read and bake pies.

CHAPTER 14

M Y SEX LIFE MIGHT HAVE taken a totally different course if I'd answered "no" to a very simple question.

I was two weeks away from graduating university and I'd taken the most boring job I could imagine. I spent eight hours on the phone every day in the basement of a suburban townhouse, which was pretty much my idea of hell, but being a focus group facilitator paid a little over minimum wage and I was consumed with fear of the upcoming joblessness and homelessness that came with graduation. So when my cellphone lit up, I was quick to respond.

Jess: My friend's band is playing downtown tonight, you wanna come?

After writing back a quick "yes," I checked my hair and makeup. Not perfect, but good enough for indie music on a Thursday night. With just one more essay left to write before I got that life-changing piece of paper, I felt a sudden thrill. This is what our lives are going to look like from now on, isn't it? Going out downtown on weekday nights because we're "friends with the band." Meeting people who don't know our entire artistic and sexual histories. Being free to go out after work because we can read whatever we want, whenever we want, and no one will expect us to write an essay about it. Despite the blond IKEA desk and flaccid headset I was currently chained to, graduation was starting to look pretty good.

I got off the streetcar where it stopped right in front of the bar and ducked inside quickly. Posters for upcoming shows and albums released on local indie record labels peppered the walls. In the dim light, everything was coloured the dark muted red of faded velvet and the dusty deep brown of old wood past its prime. The rich carpets, gone frayed and shaggy, combined with the ornate baroque paintings on the walls gave the place the look of a mid-range Victorian brothel. The band was already mid-set and the pianist was playing an old upright piano instead of the usual electric keyboard. It drove home the strange nineteenth-century feeling.

My friends were all sitting at a long table near the front with pint glasses and pitchers of beer scattered between them. I hadn't expected so many of them to make the long trip downtown, but I smiled. This was surely another sign that our lives were about to change for the better. The only seats left were right up close to the stage, so I ordered my pint and slid into the front next to Jess.

"We're going to set Dina up with someone in the band," she whispered in my ear. "But not the bass player. I want him."

I laughed. "Can I have one, too?"

"You want John?"

"Which one is he?"

"The drummer."

I looked at the band carefully for the first time. The drummer was just a few metres away from me, but I had to twist to see him between the other musicians. He looked comfortable onstage. He had a nice haircut and wore stylish clothes.

I shrugged.

"I don't know. Maybe."

I drank my beer and sank back into my chair. I didn't see what Jess saw in the bassist; he looked a little goofy to me. I watched John, but I wasn't in the mood to throw myself at anyone.

As the band started in on their last song, Jess took an empty pitcher and walked it around the bar; the money she collected in those three minutes was every penny the band would make that night. I'd like to think I threw in a five- or ten-dollar bill, but I honestly can't remember if I gave anything at all.

Jess finished her rounds and sat back down. Seconds later John appeared at her shoulder with a fresh pint.

"Thanks for doing that," he said, handing her the beer.

It seemed if anyone was going to pair up that night it would be him and Jess. But there were no empty chairs next to her and he didn't hesitate for a moment before sitting down next to me.

Talking to him was like talking to a friend I already knew fairly well, but hadn't seen in years. I don't remember much of the conversation, but I remember the feeling. Relaxed. I wasn't flirting, I wasn't trying to accomplish anything. I was just being nice to the friend-of-a-friend who turned out to be just as nice and very easy to talk to.

"I've got a gig on Friday in St. Catharines," he said casually. I must have asked him about his music … it was obvious he didn't like to talk too much about himself.

"Really? That's my hometown — sort of. I'm from a nearby little town but that's where I went to high school."

"Man. I'm sorry," he joked.

"Me too." I laughed.

"Well, you're definitely the nicest thing to come out of St. Catharines."

It reads like a line. A playboy pickup artist kind of line. But he made it sound so casual, like a joke between old friends. He said it almost ironically, making it clear that he knew it was a bit of a silly thing to say.

Slowly people started to leave. John was one of the first to go, leaving with a simple goodbye. I didn't think I'd see much of him in the future, but he was a nice new acquaintance for my nice new life. Jess and I took the long subway ride home together. Somewhere along the ride I burst into a grin.

"If only my sixteen-year-old self could see me now!"

A few days later I was putting on my makeup when I heard Jess bound down the stairs from her room giggling.

"John is going ask you out!" she said, popping her head in through the open bathroom door.

"What? How do you know?"

"Because he told me. He just messaged me and asked me if you're single and what you're into."

I smiled. I felt all fluttery inside. "What did you tell him?"

"I told him you like reading, writing, and *Pride and Prejudice*."

"Jess! You told him that?"

"Yeah! It's true, isn't it?"

"Yes, but you don't tell a *guy* that."

"Well, too late now …"

I laughed. Jess should have known better than to tell a guy you like Jane Austen.

"Anyway," she continued, "what are you going to say?"

"I dunno … I mean, if he asks me, I'll say yes, and if he doesn't, there's nothing to say."

I turned back to put on my eyeliner.

"That's it?" Jess seemed to be waiting for something more.

"Well yeah … if he asks, that's great, and if not, whatever."

● ● ● ● ●

Facebook Messenger, 6:10 p.m.

John: Hey, what are you up to this week, hang out?

Me: Hi, that sounds fun! I work until 9 every day,
but I'm free after

John: what day is good for you?

Me: I'm going out of town on Friday but other than
that any day is good! What day is best for you?

John: wed?

John: there is a good rolling stones cover band
that plays on wednesdays

Me: That sounds great!

The following Wednesday, I packed a few extra things into my purse before going to work. I chose my outfit carefully and spent extra time in the shower to make sure I didn't miss any spots when shaving my legs. My day was monotonous as usual, but there was something brewing under it all.

I hadn't been this excited for a date in months.

I hurried off from work at 9:00 p.m., right on schedule. It was a cool spring so I pulled on my leather gloves and buttoned my peacoat on my walk to the subway. I checked my phone to make sure my timing was perfect before stepping into the public bathroom at the entrance to the station. I dug into my purse and pulled out the extra makeup bag I'd prepared that morning. Careful not to let anything touch the bathroom counters, I patted a fresh coat of concealer under my eyes, refreshed my blush, and re-curled my eyelashes after adding a new coat of mascara. I topped it all off with a light layer of lipstick.

A subway, another subway, and finally I was on the bus. I checked my phone again; I was still making perfect time. I might even be a little bit early. The bus rumbled south and the neighbourhood began to look a little familiar. I checked the map on my phone. Ahh, yes. I'd been this way for a date once before. I wasn't sure if that was a good sign or a bad one.

I stepped off the bus and walked down the stairs into the basement bar. That week had turned into a whirlwind tour of Toronto's indie hot spots, but this second bar couldn't have been more different from the first with its wood-panelled walls and decor made from up-cycled barrels. The whole place screamed country-western, but the disco ball above the stage and the strings of bright incandescent lights behind the bar gave the place a gleam of glamour. It was undoubtedly hip country-chic. I took a seat at a table for two next to the wall about halfway from the stage. It was perfectly neutral. I picked the chair that put my back against the wall so I could keep one eye on the front door and be clearly visible to all new arrivals. I thought about ordering a drink, but I decided to wait for him. I scrolled through my phone and played with the ends of my hair.

I am going to have sex tonight.

How many times had I said that to myself? I had completely lost track. Fifty? A million? But this time it felt real. For the first time I didn't feel like I was giving myself false hope; I had a good feeling about this guy, about how easy and natural it had been to get to know him. I stared at my split ends and contemplated different ways to orchestrate the situation. I'd have to get him to invite me back to his place since I lived too far away. I wanted to be the perfect combination of sexy and willing, but not too available. I'd been burned before by "slut" and "whore." I was worried that if I came on too strong, I'd pigeonhole myself as too easy, or maybe even too brave.

Having sex on a first date in the twenty-first century is both okay and not okay. This is very different territory from a casual hookup after a party. A whole new set of bullshit applies when you're actually *dating* the guy. I'd been taught to beware the risks of the "sex-on-the-first-date curse."

I felt like I had to play a game, the kind of game I'd always hoped I would be above, but wasn't at all (not yet). I thought the rules were different now that John and I had at the very least adopted the pretence of dating. This wasn't going to be a drunken party hookup and I felt like I had to behave differently, to hold myself to a different standard because these were different circumstances. I couldn't just say what I wanted — "I want to go home with you" — for fear that he would think I was too forward.

Even after all this time, I couldn't be true to myself and what I wanted. Instead, I prepared to dance delicately so I could get what I wanted while trying to maintain the facade of who I thought I should be. I didn't even know yet if I would want to keep dating him, but I knew I liked talking to him and I wanted to keep that door open. The truth is I thought everyone would respect me less if I slept with him on the first date. It's an ancient paradox: be just the right amount of sexually liberated, display it in exactly the right way, and enact it only under a very specific set of circumstances.

Around the same time, a good friend of mine had been having fantastic casual sex with a guy she actually kind of liked. Not long before my date with John, the guy had told her she wasn't "girl-friend material." According to him, she had come on too strong and no longer fit the profile of the kind of girl he saw himself dating. She was another victim of the Madonna-Whore Complex. I remembered Tyler and the idea that I was "too good" for a hookup, and Kevin who called me a "nice girl," as if I couldn't be both nice and sexual at the same time. I wanted John to see me differently, but I was still struggling to let go of the past and many misguided social constructions.

Time slows down when you're early for a date and waiting for the guy to show up. Luckily it was only 10:00 p.m. and the bar was still mostly empty. John walked in looking a little different than

I remembered, but I couldn't pinpoint exactly what had changed. He wore a white V-neck T-shirt under a black leather coat and an expensive pair of jeans. A silver chain peeked out under his collar. The whole look was simple, classic, sexy.

"Hey," he said, sitting down. "Sorry if I'm a bit late."

"No, it's okay. I was early."

"You want a drink?"

"Sure," I said, reaching for my bag. This wasn't the kind of place to offer table service.

"No. No, I'll get it." He motioned for me to stay seated while he got up to go to the bar. "What do you want?"

"I'll have whatever you're having."

"I was going to have a beer."

"Beer, then. Sounds great."

"What kind of beer do you like?" he asked.

"I'll have the most boring beer."

"You want a boring beer?"

"Yeah," I said. "I like boring beer. You know, light, blond … whatever's boring."

"Okay." He nodded slowly.

He came back moments later with two pints of Molson Stock Ale. Perfect. Blond, generic, domestic, boring.

We chatted through the usual first-date conversations before the band came on, and even when the music started we didn't stop.

"Why do you have a compass on your phone?" he asked after catching a glimpse of my iPhone home screen.

"I like travel. And adventures."

"Huh." He didn't seem satisfied.

I am the master of my fate. I am the captain of my soul.

"It reminds me of … you know, something important," I continued. "Something someone said to me once."

Know nothing. Seek everything. Trust that the fire in your heart will guide you.

I smiled and nudged him playfully. "Come on, what's on your phone?"

He showed me a black-and-white photo of Marlon Brando.

"It's from *The Godfather*," he said. "Have you seen it?"

"Nope."

"Jess didn't seem to think we'd have much in common."

"I wasn't sure, either."

"Then why did you agree to come?"

"Well, I tend to make life decisions based on whether or not I think it will make a good story."

"Whether or not it will make a good story. Huh."

"Yup. Pretty much."

"Do you want to dance?" he asked.

I hesitated. I didn't normally dance without a lot more alcohol.

"Let's go stand closer so we can see the band," he suggested. "You don't have to dance if you don't want to."

Leaving my coat behind on my chair, we got up to stand at the edge of the crowd near the bar. He reached out and touched the hem of my shirt gently.

"I like your shirt," he said. He was standing close to me now. I looked up at him, and the lights behind the bar twinkled as he leaned down ever so slightly to kiss me. Soft, sweet, simple. It only lasted the briefest of moments before I opened my eyes and smiled. With his arms around me, I turned to face the band and started to dance a little bit. His hands on my hips drummed lightly in time to the music.

"You're a good dancer," he said in my ear. I simply smiled again, knowing that's what guys always say.

The band played on, every Rolling Stones hit I knew, and many I had never heard before. I checked the time subtly: 1:15

a.m. If I didn't leave right that second, I would miss the last subway train home. I put my phone back in my pocket and kept
dancing. The band launched into their final song and shouts of
"Last call!" sprung up across the room.

We stayed until the guitar cables had all been coiled and the last
sips of beer had been drunk before climbing the stairs together back
into the cool fresh air. The bus stop glimmered right in front of us.
I looked at my phone and pretended to be surprised by the time.

"Oh, no, I missed the last subway."

"What are you going to do?"

"My dad lives downtown; I'll just go crash at his place."

"Where does he live?"

"West."

"Me too; want me to walk you?"

"Sure. It's pretty far, but I'll walk a little ways."

We walked together through deserted streets; it seemed like
the whole city was quiet and sleeping. I tugged on the ends of my
gloves as we walked, suddenly very aware that they weren't quite
the right colour to match my coat.

"Do you want to walk the whole way?" he asked.

"No, I'll get on the streetcar eventually. I can't believe I lost
track of time!"

Why hasn't he asked me to go home with him?

"I mean," I continued, "I thought that might happen ... but I
knew I could just stay at my dad's ..."

"Or ..." He hesitated, but he was smiling. "You could stay at
my place if you want."

He reached out slowly to put his arm around me. He let
his hand rest lightly on my shoulder and kept his body an arm's
length away.

My fear of seeming too eager prompted me to hesitate.

"I don't know ... *mayyybee* ... let's keep walking."

I wondered what he was thinking. Did he subscribe to these patriarchal ideas I was so afraid would shame me? Would anything I did in the next hour change the opinion he had made of me over the last four?

But it had been ten years since André had passed me that note in the tennis ball and I was so fucking tired. All I wanted was to be liberated enough to make my own choices about my body, secure in the knowledge that, whatever happened next, I would have no regrets because I'd made my own decision.

We kept wandering west until John stopped on a corner.

"I'm just down here." He pointed south. "Do you want me to wait with you for a cab or do you want to come?"

I stared into the bright yellow light above the convenience store across the street. I was sure. I knew what I wanted and I knew I wouldn't wish myself back in the morning.

"All right," I said. "Let's go."

His bedroom was clean. Clean-clean-clean. It was furnished simply, with an emphasis on the essentials: bed, desk, television, CDs galore. I took off my coat and stood in the middle of the room, pretending to read the album titles. He wandered over to turn on the TV.

"Oh, *Entourage* is on. That's a good show. Have you seen it?"

"No."

I was standing next to him now. He faced the TV and I faced him. I looked up at his ear.

"But I've heard it's good."

He kissed me again and I wrapped my arms around him.

If you want to turn back, I thought, *this is the moment*.

But I didn't.

I didn't want to.

All the issues I'd spent the last ten years agonizing over didn't matter anymore. This moment wasn't about feminism, sexual liberation, or my sense of self-worth. It wasn't about fitting in or being popular or beautiful. It wasn't about living up to the expectations I had for myself or the visions of who I thought I wanted to be.

It was simply about the fact that I liked the way his lips felt when he kissed me. I liked the way he looked at me, and the funny, intelligent things he had to say. I liked the way I felt when I was with him and I liked the way he treated me.

I liked that he didn't question my decisions or try to make this moment something other than what I wanted it to be. Unlike the other men before him, he understood that what I choose to do with my body does not have to be a political statement or a defining character trait.

A few moments later, I was no longer a virgin.

"Are you okay?" he asked, even though I'd given him no reason to think otherwise.

"Yes."

It felt oddly familiar. Unsurprising.

"You okay?" he asked again a little later, checking in with me to make sure.

I didn't know yet what to ask for, but I was more than okay. Mostly because he'd asked. And asked again.

When we were done, I was careful to lie firmly on my side of the bed, but he put his arm around me and pulled me close so I could rest my head on his shoulder.

"I should go," I said.

"It's late. Stay."

"I'll stay for a minute, but then I'm going home."

I wanted to feel powerful. I wasn't going to reinforce the archaic stereotype that sex, for a woman, is always, inherently meaningful or that all virgins become attached to their first lover. Going home meant I was in control, that I didn't need a man, that my heart doesn't live in my vagina.

I fell asleep with my head still on his shoulder.

I woke up an hour later even more resolved to leave.

"Time to go home," I told him.

"Stay. I mean —" He cut himself off, not wanting to seem like he was telling me what to do. "Whatever you want — but I'd like you to stay."

"No, not tonight."

It was 5:30 a.m. and dark outside. He got up and walked me to his front door where I hailed a cab. He kissed me goodbye.

"That was fun," he said. "I'll call you."

"Yeah. Call me. That'd be nice."

I figured the odds were fifty-fifty. I hoped he would call, but I expected him not to. The memories of all those boys I'd kissed were strong and powerful. I got into my cab and watched the sun rise all along the ride home.

I didn't know what would happen next, but I didn't have sex with John because I wanted him to be my boyfriend. I didn't have sex with him because I thought it would give me validation or because it would fit the image of my best self. I had sex with him because I wanted to.

When I woke up the next morning, a text message from John had already come in. It wasn't long before he and I were officially — casually — dating. Not much later, I asked him what he thought about me "giving it up" on the first date.

"I don't know, I didn't really think anything about it."

Boom.

There it is: the perfect answer.

Maybe having sex on the first date will change how certain men might think of you, but those are the kind of small-minded guys you definitely don't want to hang around with. My story with John is just one example of how you *can* in fact divorce your sex life and your sexual identity from your sense of self. De-emphasizing that connection and finding a guy who did the same was how I finally found the liberation I'd been looking for all along.

A few days later, I told this story to a friend.

"Congratulations!" he said. "You had sex! How do you feel?"

I paused. Was I supposed to feel different? Was I supposed to feel anything at all? Or was I supposed to *be* different? To have changed? I guess I thought I was. All those boys and all those kisses, all those magazines and feminist theories and books and stories and fairy tales led me to think that sex was something magical. Transformative. Necessary. That I would be happier, healthier, prettier, more popular, and all-around *better* if I were sexually active. But nothing was different at all.

"How do you feel?"

I caught a glimpse of my reflection in the mirror behind his head. Brown hair, pale skin, blue eyes, a smile that's always just a little too wide.

"I feel like I had sex."

EPILOGUE

I'M WINDOW-SHOPPING in the nice part of Paris on a perfect summer day. Walking down a wide boulevard off the Champs-Élysées, I see a father and son turn the corner and stroll toward me. The man is tall and Old Hollywood–handsome. The boy is all smiles and wild, curly hair. I smile back as he scampers toward me. That was my mistake. Before I know it, the man is standing right in front of me.

"I find you very sexy," he says.

Oh my god, I'm going to get chopped up and left in a dark French alley.

"Do you want to go somewhere?" he asks.

I lift my chin slightly and stand up straight. I can almost match his height, but my gaze keeps faltering. It's like trying to speak to a man with two heads and look him directly in the eye. The little boy keeps pulling my focus. He is the second head. The thing that made the situation so improbably wrong.

I shift my hands so they cover the English title of the guidebook I'm holding and I recite some version of the line all young women know to use when they're alone.

"I have somewhere to be. I'm already late. My friends are waiting for me."

I have no friends on this side of the Atlantic, but what I love most about Paris is that I'm alone.

Later that evening, I wander out of my hotel in the Latin Quarter with my notebook in hand. I've seen everything for the day. I'm tired of museums and monuments, and I'm still trying to shake off the idea that I got solicited for sex in front of Prada.

I float on my now familiar raft of solitude and imagine I am a writer from the city's Literary Golden Age. I stroll through the market on rue Mouffetard, past the fromageries and boulangeries, looking for the place. I spy a dark doorway and can glimpse little wooden tables and soft benches on the other side. It's empty. It's perfect. In Canada, it would have been called a dive bar. In Paris, it was romantic, the kind of place to inspire creative genius.

I sit at the back, tucked into a corner as far as possible from the door. I order a tiny glass of Côtes du Rhône and start to work. I'm only a few sips into my wine when a group of locals tumble in.

They crack a few jokes with the bartender and a few of the boys run back and forth past my table in and out of the kitchen. Finally they settle by the window, still chattering and joking as they order. I try to keep my eyes on my work, but I have already been pulled firmly into their orbit.

They all look about my age and impossibly cool in that effortless French way. Suddenly I feel lonely. I want to laugh and smoke and kiss my friends once on each cheek. I start wishing they would ask me to join them. I imagine all the funny things I would say. The jokes they would make about my Canadian accent. The way it would feel to go home with a French boy.

Some of them must have noticed me watching because it isn't long before one of the boys saunters up to my little corner.

I had already decided he was their leader; he was talking the loudest, waving his arms wildly, and calling out to the bartender from across the room. But when he comes over to me, he speaks softly. "A little book and a little glass of wine."

"Yes," I say.

I want to run my hands through his brown curls and hold on tightly.

"You look like someone who squeezes on the bottom of the toothpaste tube," he says, "so that you get every bit of toothpaste out."

"Well, what's wrong with that?" I reply. "If you don't squeeze on the tube, you'll just end up wasting toothpaste."

"People who squeeze on the tube are like people who try to plan love. You can't plan love."

ACKNOWLEDGEMENTS

I AM ETERNALLY GRATEFUL to my agent, Hilary McMahon, at Westwood Creative Artists, who never stopped believing in this book. You would not be holding it in your hands without her unflagging support and encouragement.

Thank you to Kathryn Lane, Shannon Whibbs, Elena Radic, Laura Boyle, Stephanie Ellis, Elham Ali, Rachel Spence, Saba Eitizaz, Lisa Marie Smith, and the entire team at Dundurn Press, who helped turn my little manuscript into a book.

Every Boy I Ever Kissed first came to life as part of the MFA in Creative Nonfiction program at the University of King's College. Thank you to my professors and mentors, Lorri Neilsen Glenn, Lori A. May, David Hayes, Don Sedgwick, and Stephen Kimber, as well as to our visiting writers and editors, for sharing their knowledge and supporting this project from day one. Thank you to my MFA classmates, who were all an essential part of this journey. Special thanks to the members of our Toronto writing group: Mary Jane Grant, Pamela Oakley, Christian Smith, and Gillian Turnbull.

Thank you to everyone along the way who generously shared their stories and experiences with me.

I wouldn't be a writer without the support of my parents and large blended family, whom I cannot thank enough. Thank you to my mother, who gave me my love of books and who has always been my first editor and loudest cheerleader.

Finally, thank you to Alan, for always making sure I have a room of my own.

NOTES

INTRODUCTION

1. Genna Buck, "Study Shows Millennials Are Having Less Sex," *Toronto Star*, February 14, 2017, thestar.com/life/2017/02/14/study-shows-millennials-are-having-less-sex.html.

CHAPTER 4

1. Elisabeth Garber-Paul, "Canada's Teens Are Increasingly Abstinent," *Rewire.News*, April 15, 2009, rewire.news/article/2009/04/15/canadas-teens-increasingly-abstinent/.
2. Erin Anderssen, "Abstinence-Only Programs Can Delay Teen Sex," *Globe and Mail*, February 2, 2010, theglobeandmail.com/life/parenting/abstinence-only-programs-can-delay-teen-sex/article571686/.
3. Ibid.
4. Jennifer Stevens Aubrey, Elizabeth Behm-Morawitz, and Melissa A. Click, "The Romanticization of Abstinence: Fan Response to Sexual Restraint in the Twilight Series," *Transformative Works and Culture* 5 (2010). transformativeworks.org/index.php/twc/article/view/216/184.

5. "Frequently Asked Questions," True Love Revolution, hcs
   .harvard.edu/tlr/faq.php.
6. Ibid.
7. Randall Patterson, "Students of Virginity," *New York
   Times*, March 30, 2008, nytimes.com/2008/03/30/
   magazine/30Chastity-t.html?em&ex=1207108800&en=13ab-
   4235900007b8&ei=5087&_r=0&mtrref=undefined&g-
   wh=1AB480C04B4A47CBCF8D2132778A6636&gwt=pay.
8. Carrie Weisman, "Virgin America: Why Young Adults Are
   Having a Hard Time Getting Laid," *Salon*, February 27, 2017,
   salon.com/2017/02/26/virgin-america-why-young-adults-are-
   having-a-hard-time-getting-laid/.

CHAPTER 6
1. Jane Austen, *Pride and Prejudice* (1813; repr., London:
   Penguin Books, 2003), 55.

CHAPTER 7
1. Kaarina Nikunen, "Cosmo Girls Talk: Blurring Boundaries
   of Porn and Sex," in *Pornification: Sex and Sexuality in
   Media Culture*, Kaarina Nikunen, Susanna Paasonen, Laura
   Saarenmaa, eds. (London: Bloomsbury, 2007), researchgate.
   net/publication/264521361_Cosmo_Girls_Talk_Blurring_
   boundaries_of_porn_and_sex.
2. Charles Kirkpatrick, Steve Duck, and Megan K. Foley,
   eds., *Relating Difficulty: The Processes of Constructing and
   Managing Difficult Interaction* (New York, NY: Routledge,
   2013), 144.
3. Ibid., 145.
4. "101. Sex and the City (Pilot)," Sex and the City Transcripts,
   satctranscripts.com/2008/08/sex-and-city-season-1-episode-
   1.html#.W_FU1GOYeFJ.

5. Kathleen A. Bogle, *Hooking Up: Sex, Dating, and Relationships on Campus* (New York: New York University Press), 33.

6. Ibid., 9.

7. Zosia Bielski, "The Sex Myth: Why You Shouldn't Assume Everyone Is Having Better Sex Than You," *Globe and Mail*, September 24, 2015, theglobeandmail.com/life/ relationships/sex-positivitys-dark-side-why-you-should-nt-assume-everyone-is-having-better-sex-than-you/ article26519767/.

8. Kathleen A. Bogle, *Hooking Up: Sex, Dating, and Relationships on Campus* (New York: New York University Press), 5.

9. Ibid., 59.

10. Ibid., 59.

11. Mitchell J. Prinstein, Christina S. Meade, Geoffrey L. Cohen, "Adolescent Oral Sex, Peer Popularity, and Perceptions of Best Friends' Sexual Behavior," *Journal of Pediatric Psychology* 28, no. 4 (June 2003): 243–49, jpepsy.oxfordjournals.org/content /28/4/243.full.

CHAPTER 8

1. Jessica Eaton, "Why I don't want women to become 'equal to men,'" *Victimfocus* (blog), August 4, 2018, victimfocus .wordpress.com/2018/08/04/why-i-dont-want-to-become-equal-to-men/.

CHAPTER 9

1. Zosia Bielski, "For Those Who Wait, There's a Risk of Stigma, Experts Say," *Globe and Mail*, October 22, 2009, theglobeandmail.com/life/health-and-fitness/health/condi-tions/for-those-who-wait-theres-a-risk-of-stigma-experts-say/ article572661.

2. Ibid.

3. Laura M. Carpenter, "Gender and the Meaning and Experience of Virginity Loss in the Contemporary United States," *Gender & Society* 16, no. 3 (2002): 345–65.

4. Ibid., 358.

5. Anna North, "How Guys Feels About Sex with Virgins," *Jezebel*, January 13, 2012, jezebel.com/5875854/how-guys-feel-about-sex-with-virgins.

6. Shannon Najamabadi, "Hookup: The Stigma Surrounding Virginity," *Daily Californian*, May 28, 2012, dailycal .org/2012/05/28/hook-up-the-stigma-surrounding-virginity.

CHAPTER 10

1. Kristina-Anne Gylling, "It Happened to Me: I Tried to Have Sex with My Gay Male Best Friend," xojane, August 13, 2012, xojane.com/it-happened-to-me/it-happened-me-i-tried-have-sex-my-gay-male-best-friend.

2. Francesca Gaiba, "Straight women and gay men friends: A qualitative study" (Ph.D. diss., Syracuse University, 2007).

CHAPTER 11

1. Dr. Hernando Chaves, "Overcoming Performance Anxiety," AskMen, askmen.com/dating/love_tip_60/79_love_tip.html.

2. Larry O'Connor, "Sexual Performance Anxiety in Men," Larry O'Connor, MFT, June 12, 2012, larryoconnor.info/archives/lo_articles/sexual-performance-anxiety.

3. Ramin Setoodeh, "Not That Into You: Wrong Advice for Obama Era," *Newsweek*, February 4, 2009, newsweek.com/not-you-wrong-advice-obama-era-82415.

4. "50% of British Guys in Their Thirties Admit They Suffer from Erectile Dysfunction," Atomik Research, atomikresearch .co.uk/50-of-male-brits-in-their-30s-suffer-erectile-problems.

5. Larry O'Connor, "Sexual Performance Anxiety in Men."

6. "Male Sexual Performance Anxiety," National Social Anxiety Center, nationalsocialanxietycenter.com/social-anxiety/male-sexual-performance-anxiety.

7. Larry O'Connor, "Sexual Performance Anxiety in Men."

CHAPTER 12

1. Gillian Flynn, *Gone Girl* (New York: Broadway Books), 222.

2. *Chelsea*, episode 8, "Perils of Porn & Rachel Bloom's Big Year," written by Adam De La Peña, Netflix, aired May 26, 2016.

3. Dan Savage, "All Men Watch Porn (But Not All Men Murder Their Wives and Children)," *The Stranger*, February 7, 2012, thestranger.com/slog/archives/2012/02/07/all-men-watch-porn.

4. Noah B.E. Church, *Wack: Addicted to Internet Porn* (Seattle: Bvrning Qvestions, 2014), 9.

5. Dr. Norman Doidge, *The Brain That Changes Itself* (New York: Viking Press, 2007), 71.

6. r/NoFap, reddit, reddit.com/r/NoFap.

7. r/NoFap, "Just checked out r/fetish it is fucking disgusting to see where I came from and where I am now," reddit, March 5, 2017, reddit.com/r/NoFap/comments/5xr3ck.

8. r/NoFap, "Female Object" reddit, March 6, 2017, reddit.com/r/NoFap/comments/5xs17c.

CHAPTER 13

1. AskMen, "Men, is 'being masculine' a big part of your life or self image? What is your main method of feeling manly (Gym, sports, drinking with friends, etc) 2016, reddit.com/r/AskMen/comments/3x27y3/men_is_being_masculine_a_big_part_of_your_life_or/.